World Music Compilation

Combines:

World Music Class (2015)
Vincent Trio Scores (2015)
Soul + Salsa = Soulsa (2015)
Barry's Songs I (2015)

Written, Produced & Published
by
Teo Vincent IV
of
Givnology
Wellness Arts
Charmony Division

─────── GIVNOLOGY ───────

To assist harmony and tempo, balance and beauty.

All rights reserved.

Vincent IV, Teo (Barry)
World Music Compilation
p. cm.
Includes Music glossary, classical scores made easy and step by step Afro-Latin / Caribbean percussion lessons.
ISBN 978-1479110162 (pbk.)
1. Science of Sound 2. Harmony Basics 3. Afro-Latin-Caribbean Percussion Lessons. 4. African-American Contributions to Music 5. World Music songs & percussion arrangements 6. Yoruba Tribe from Nigeria, Africa, Orisha deities' sacred songs 7. Inspirations from the Master Composers 8. Motifs, motives & perpetual motivations 9. Affirmations & positive message music 10. Classical songs rearranged for bass-piano-violin trio
 I. Title.
2012

Music / Reference

Teo Vincent IV is a technical writer and composer from Berkeley, California. He studies at the Royal Conservatory of Music and piano privately with Oszkar Morzsa of the Franz Liszt Academy in Budapest, Hungary. He continues learning, composing, arranging, inventing, teaching, creating education & wellness new-media.

A really big special thanks to George *"Thurgopedia"* Thurgood at the RCM (Royal Conservatory of Music) for his encouragement, academic excellence, expert teaching skills, piano & creative collaboration.

Thanks to Oszkar Morzsa for sharing his virtuosic finesse, piano teaching & great knowledge of music of the world.

Thanks to IMSLP.org (go donate to them!) for song collection organizing standards. Paintings by Inda Sabatini.

Our Charmony Series:
1) Honoring Those That Went Before, Classical and World Music Piano Scores. 2) World Music Class, The Aspire Higher Project. 3) Vincent Trio Scores. 4) Soul + Salsa = Soulsa. 5) Barry's Songs I. 6) How To Be In Harmony.

http://givnology.ca has the latest files!

World Music Compilation
ISBN-13: 978-1479110162
ISMN: 979-0-9001443-6-2
BISAC: Music / Reference

© 2012 Givnology Wellness Arts, Charmony Division

World Music Class (2015)
The Aspire Higher Project

⇒ Science of Sound — 4
- Sound is vibrations — 4
  - Sound has: Amplitude, Quality and Pitch — 4
  - Scale and Key — 4
- **Notation – What are all those little dots, lines and squiggles?** — 4
  - Diagram of parts of a musical note — 4
  - Time is Horizontal, Harmony is Vertical — 6
- **Letter Names Of Notes On Instruments** — 7
  - Piano and Keyboards — 7
  - Note Letter Names on **String** Instruments — 7
    - Guitar — 7
    - String Instrument Family — 8
- **How to Find the Notes for a Song** — 8
- **How to Teach Yourself to Read Short Music Scores** — 9
  - Twinkle Twinkle Little Star / Baa Baa Black Sheep / ABCs — 9
- **Intervals Between Notes** — 9
  - Basic Intervals on the Treble Clef — 11
    - Table of Intervals & numbers of Semitones & Whole Tones — 11
    - Intervals going up and down — 12
  - Intervals Add Up To Chords — 12
- **Ranges and Transpositions** — 12
  - Instrument Ranges & Transposing for them — 13
- **The Circle of Fifths** — 14
  - Circle of Fifths on the Keyboard — 15
- **Key Signatures** — 16
  - Minor Key Signatures — 17
- **Harmonics** — 18
  - The Harmonic Series — 18
- **The Science of Harmonics** — 19
  - Tuning with harmonics / overtones — 19
  - Playing "Revile" with harmonic overtones — 19
  - Sine and Square waves, the mouth as a filter — 19
- **Greek Modes or Scales** — 19
  - Harmonic Minor Dominant – (Flamenco / Middle Eastern / Phrygian Dominant / Freygish) — 20
- **World Music Mastery, Building Blocks for Playing With Anyone!** — 21
- **Common Chords** — 22
  - Triads, chords that are 1 – 3 – 5 — 22
  - Seventh Chords 1 – 3 – 5 – 7 — 23
- **Heuristic Music Learning** — 25
  - Be A Useful Member Of Your Music Projects — 26
- **Fine Playing on Keyboard** — 26
  - What you *CAN* learn on keyboards: — 27
    - FINE PLAYING techniques when you have access to a real piano: — 28
- **MIDI = Music Instrument Digital Interface (5 pin din plug)** — 28
- **Review of Chords** — 29
  - Extended chords = 1 - 3 - 5 - 7 - 9 - 11 - 13 — 29

⇒ Percussionist Roles — 30
- Overview: Instruments' names *are* their roles — 30
- **Clavitos, Claves For Beginners** — 30
- **Clave Offenders** — 31
- **Percs1: Da-dada-da-da** — 31
- **Percs2: Clave Down! & Percs3: Son Clave + Pulse** — 32
- **Percs4: Palito (Simple and Basic) & Percs5: Clave & Palito in Binary (back and forth)** — 33
- **Percs6: Rumba Clave, Palito & Binary & Percs7: Rumba Palito** — 34
- **Percs8: Rumba Clave & Rumba Palito in Binary** — 35
- **Percs9: Rumba Palito in 2-3 and Conga Dance** — 35
- **Percs10: 6/8 Agogo & Cowbell Patterns** — 36
- **Percs20: Entries – "Counting In" With Sides** — 37
- **Percs21: Endings – Outtros in Unison** — 37
  - Brazilian Unison Outtro — 37
- **Percs22: Hearing Songs' Claves & Sides** — 38
- **World Music Stories** — 38
- **Percussion Patterns Made into Melodic Phrases** — 38
- **World Music Definitions of Afro-Latin Music Percussion Roles & Rules** — 39
- **Complimenting Ensembles** — 45
- **Highlife has: 1-Rhythm, 2-Line and 3-Lead Guitar Parts** — 45
- **Rhythm Section Accompaniment "Chucks"** — 47
- **The *Yoruba* People from Nigeria, West Africa** — 51
  - Some *Afro-Latin Music* definitions: — 51

⇒ Motifs and Motivations — 52
- Beethoven't 5th becomes a Perpetual Motivator — 52
- Call and Response / Rhythmic Balance in Latin Music — 52
- **Afro-American Contributions** — 52
  - All About The Bass — 53

Perpetual Motivations	**53**
The Montuno is a Great Motorvator	54
TIGHT SCHOOL	**59**
Review: The Correct Side Of The Pattern	59
Tres Golps (3 gulps or 3 pulses)	59
CHUCKS (Accompaniment Accenting One or the Other Side)	60
DESIGNING MONTUNOS	60
Sections, Unions & Oppositions	**62**
Louisiana style **Second-Line** chants calls and answers	62
Phrases	**63**
What's the *Catch-Phrase*	63
High Life Phrasing	63
Hohner D-6 Clavinet	64
When you can use Motorvations:	65
Motives, motifs and motivational inspiring	66
Giving credit	**66**
Yradier's-Bizet's-Carmen's Habanera	66
Create a Time Capsule for the Future	67
Affirmatinas – Positive Message Music	**67**
Affirmation Songs	**70**
Lyrics of "Pati, to Patience" and "Silent Tears"	71
Positive Messages on Classical Derivatives	**72**
Inspirations from The Masters	**75**
Music is the Universal Language	77
Glossary of Italian Musical Terms for Performance Instruction	**106**
⇒ **The Total Musical Piece**	**107**
"Carmen" Caribbean Rumba Percussion Parts with Coro adapted to teach percussion	108
"Yemaya" & "Santa Lucia" Bembe Agogo & Drum Patterns with Coros	110

Table of Scores

Twinkle Twinkle Little Star / Baa Baa Black Sheep / ABCs	9
Form Figure No. 1, Resolmilafatimila. Elegant yet simple sequence / circle of 5^{ths}. A foundation for improvisation or ensemble work	20
World Music Mastery, Building blocks for playing with anyone! Standard I-IV-V progressions, beginner to advanced	21
Bars 30-32 of Praelude No. 1 by J.S. Bach – study of Seventh Suspended chords	24
Latin Piano (Montuno) 101: "La Bamba" C I-IV-V-IV major and minor (with I-ii-V-ii variation)	24
Montuno Etude #0, Montuno Circles Makes Blues Scale, Shekere pattern as piano montuno	38
Yoruba Diasporas, Rumba Parts translated into Melodic Phrases	40
Calypso Study in Soca (Soul-Calypso) often the first side (bar) is Up and the second half is Down	46
Yemaya Orisha Ocean Goddess, Sacred Song of the Nigerian Yoruba Tribe	48
Syncro-Nice Sacred Rhythm Scales, Major and Lydian Scales Sync with Sacred West-African Percussion	54
Conversation Pieces: Extremely Potent Repeatable Perpetual Motivations	54
Montuno Etude #1, Primer for First Time Montuno (Latin Piano) Technique	55
Swing Montuno Study, 6/8 Swing Jazz, Montuno Rhythmic Tension added to the Melodic Role	56
Montuno Etude #2, "That Makes This Heaven" C Major 1-VI-ii-V Montuno and Bajo Tumbau (Bass)	58
Calypso Circles circles of fifths with calypso chuck (downbeat on the first half version)	62
Clavinet Keyboard Score 1,"Soca Clav" Soul-Calypso standard keyboard chuck	64
Clavinet Keyboard Score 2,"Superclav" Super Clavinet Technique	65
Affirmatinas: "Everything's going perfectly, now and ever more!" "Having what I'm wanting, wanting what I'm having."	67
Bossanova Study, Sweet Love Song, Piano, Chords & Lyrics: "Lost In Love"	68
Affirmatina Song, Piano and Lyrics: "My Successes Are Here"	70
Classical Derivative Affirmatina #1, "I Manifest My Destiny" based on Chopin Mazurka in C	73
Classical Derivative Affirmatina #2, "Chopin Made A Way" based on Chopin's C# minor waltz	74
Classical Derivative Affirmatina #3, "Let It Be's" based on Abbe Franz Liszt's "Liebestraum"	75
Chamber Concertoo in D Major, RV 93, Antonio Vivaldi, reduction to piano and guitar chords	80
Che Farò Senza Euridice?, Christoph Willibald Gluck, theme reduction to piano solo	82
Winter from The 4 Seasons, Antonio Vivaldi, reduction to piano and guitar chords	83
• Canto: The Triumph of Truth & Time (later the opera Rinaldo), George Frederic Handel, reduction to piano, chords and vocals	84
Les Baricades Misterieuses, by Francois Couperin, adapted to modern piano and sustain pedal	86
• Canto: Gelido in Ogni Vena, from the opera Farnace by Antonio Vivaldi, reduction to piano, chords and vocals	88
Song To The Moon from the opera Rusalka, by Antonin Dvorak, thematic reduction to piano and chords	91
Clarinet Concerto in A Major, the Adagio, by Wolfgang Amadeus Mozart, reduction to piano solo	92
• Canto: Laudate Dominum, Wolfgang Amadeus Mozart, reduction to piano, chords and Latin vocals	94
• Canto: The Magic Flute, The Priest's Aria, reduction to piano, lyrics and chords	97
• Canto: Ave Maria (originally Ellens Gesang for Sir Walter Scott poems) by Franz Schubert, piano, chords and Latin vocals	98
• Bel Canto: Casta Diva from the opera Norma, by Vincenzo Bellini, reduction to piano, chords and vocals	100
Andante Moderato from Symphony #9, by Ludwig Van Beethoven, reduction to piano solo	102
Adagio from Symphony #1 by Georges Bizet, reduction to piano solo	103
Romeo and Juliet Overture, Pyotr Tchaikovsky, Theme Reduction by Teo Vincent IV	104
Andalucia, by Ernesto Lecuona, reduction to piano, chords and melody	105
Percs Score 1, Carmen – Carmen's Habanera, Clave, Percussion, Coro (Chorus) adapted to teach the percussion patterns	108
Percs Score 2, Yemaya & Santa Lucia, Agogo, Percussion, Coro (Chorus) in Yoruba and English	110

The next set of books starts on page 113 with another table of contents

How To Use "World Music Class"

There are at least as many perspectives on the truth as there are people on Earth. Some people believe good music is a groove, a repeated beat and bass with a chant. Others see music as timeless – without tempo – huge structures that reach up to infinity in harmony and resonation. "World Music Class" combines how to make excellent repetitive rhythmic patterns and also helps you understand chords, melodies, harmony and "High Art" music.

This book first began as a documenting of knowledge gathered from many years of experience. It now shares both the technical knowledge of music creation: composition and production, and also helpful tips passed to you from years of performance in groups small and large, to a wide range of audiences, *sit-down* to *get-down*.

You will learn how to see the little Clave sticks' key important role in rhythmic arrangement. "World Music Class" is also a very comprehensive reference of most basic music fundamentals, instrument and vocal ranges, instrument tunings, transpositions, keys and so on. You will find many helpful shortcuts, cheat-sheets, simplifications and clear diagrams to assist you. Also, stories about the artists and cultures keeps you entertained and inspired to learn.

Mid-way through the book we share stories and lessons we can all learn from the master composers and the history of this amazing art form: music. Toward the end of the book we have compiled an exhaustive selection of classical standards with optional accompaniment chords, and finally a few extra-ordinary pieces that are well known classics re-engineered to include and teach percussion patterns, therefore merging European music histories and non-western music histories such as African rhythmic patterns, clearly diagrammed on the same scores!

"World Music Class" can help you:

- **Play together in many various ways** (many enjoyable songs are made easier to play together on by means of including optional accompaniment guitar chords and thematic reductions).

- **Learn Grandma's song so that family members can have the ancient and never-out-of-style joy of playing family favorites together** (fun techniques to write down songs you hear and write scores).

- **Break from traditions in the correct way: know the traditions and their rules, then learn how to respectfully modernize in non-insulting ways** (many loved classics to study are in this one volume).

"World Music" often means Non-Western or Non-Academic (Non-Literate). Then the composer Franz Liszt put Gypsy songs into orchestrations. Mozart has a Turkish Sonata. Many composers borrowed from other cultures such as Brahms, Handel, and Bizet. Many forms have traveled around such as Rumba, Tango, Czardas (a Hungarian form pronounced: Chardash), and Habanera (a seductive song form from Havana, Cuba). We give you the tools to dissect and transform songs and music from one place and merge it into another. Please be polite and remember that *quality is not quantity*. Be sparing and see the spaces between notes as important as the notes themselves!

If you find 8 bars of a song you like, repeat that until you are satisfied! Then try the next section. Being able to improvise your curriculum is a great joy. Students should be allowed to flip through this book, then learn about what inspires them! *Practicing what you love motivates for the hours that are needed.*

Hopefully this book is received with the same positive intention it is shared with and all the types of musical learning and enjoying are catalyzed, encouraged and enhanced. ***This book is great for self-study, and classes!***

Activities that can be done in the classroom are shown like this

Homework & practicing exercises are shown like this

Science of Sound

Sound is vibrations

Sound is vibrations that go in your ear and move your eardrums, moving amniotic fluid inside your ear and ganglia in the ear canal register the vibrations and send signals to the brain that computes what it is and where it is in relation to you.

Sound has: Amplitude, Quality and Pitch

- **Amplitude** or volume or loudness or intensity, measured in decibels (Alexander Graham Bell 1847-1922).
- **Quality** is parameters such as percussiveness, tambre ("oo" or "ee"), harmonic fullness (pure operatic voice or growl of Flamenco or Blues), repetitions.
- **Pitch** which has highness or lowness, **making the sound a tone**.

Highness or lowness depends on frequency, literally how often is the vibration.

Make 1 vibration per second on something, like clapping. Try 4 times per second, and be accurate. That is 4 Hz (Henrich Hertz 1857-1894). Play 4 Hz in one hand and the offbeats in the other. Now you are playing 8 Hz. Could you imagine someone playing 16 Hz? Some percussionists play this and even faster!

Audible Tones

Tones most of us hear are between 20 Hz and 20,000 Hz. Dogs hear above this elephants below. Lower sounds have a long wave. The bass tones you turn up with the tone knob on your stereo you can't hear right at the speaker but your neighbor does!!!

Scale and Key

A song can be in any key. From any note you sing or make, you call it the Do or beginning of a scale. Sing *ANY* note. Now sing the same note and start the song: "Doe, a deer, a female deer.." You can sing the Do-re-mi scale on any note or pitch.

Have students find any pitch (key) they like. Have them sing "Do re me fa so la ti do." Tell them do to do is an octave, as is re to re, etc.. Octave means 8 notes. After they are done, tell them what key they were in, have them remember it – maybe it's "their key!"

Joke: The middle sea is the <u>Atlantic</u> – or the <u>Pacific</u> for Asians.

Notation – What are all those little dots, lines and squiggles?

Diagram of parts of a musical note

Flags (beams if connected to other notes) →

Note Stem →

Note Head →

Notes on a musical staff have lengths, how long the note is held. Also the rests between notes have lengths or TIME VALUES. Here are the main ones to know:

LENGTH	NOTE SYMBOL	REST SYMBOL
WHOLE NOTE	𝅝	𝄻
HALF NOTE	𝅗𝅥	𝄼
QUARTER NOTE	♩	𝄽
EIGHTH NOTE	♪	𝄾
SIXTEENTH NOTE	𝅘𝅥𝅯	𝄿

As you can see from the following, **One whole note equals two half notes**. Two quarter notes equals a half note. Two 16th notes equals one quarter note. It goes on and on.

The same is true of rests. You will see notes and rests mixed up in musical scores, but it all has to add up!

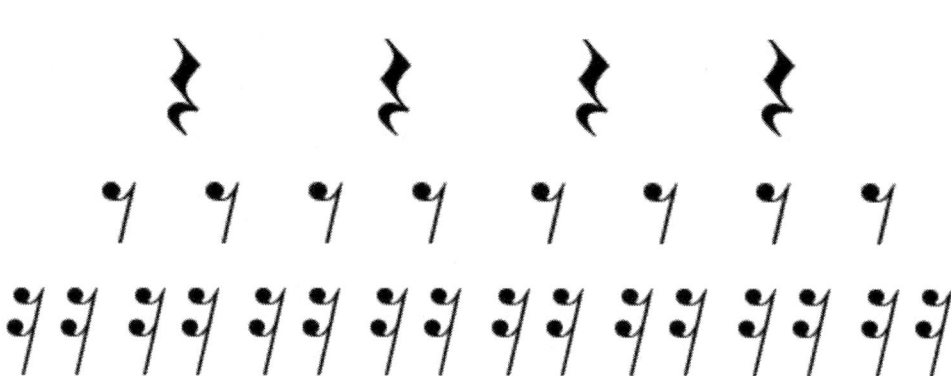

Time is Horizontal, Harmony is Vertical

Tempo → Time goes from left to right

TEMPO – Horizontal

Practice how your ear hears TIME. Try playing along with a recording and singing or listening along, then turn the player off for a few seconds and see if when you turn it back up you are in the right part of the song. This is testing and tuning / timing up your internal clock, your internal rhythm (of course your subconscious knows all these things, human brains manage the rhythms of hundreds of functions constantly). It's just a tuning in to your internal clocks, and learning how to give them wonderful tools to make yourself more accurate in your timing.

A great tool for this is the good old metronome, or what most SEQUENCER programs have set as the CLICK TRACK. Use a metronome or record a rhythm / click track and play along. Many professional artists can't play along with a click track. Hopefully you can hear the click or pulse in your head, hear where others might be dragging or rushing the time, hear where you want to be on the time, and in "real-time" help the other musicians get right into the time AND feel while still being impeccably in time yourself. *Solo performance is more flexible*.

You can usually change the instruments of these click tracks, the main thing is to play them loudly while you play loudly - and record and listen back to make sure and critically check where your rhythmic and timing weaknesses might be. Time and tune yourself up and be the tightest musician in your area rhythmically and the universe will hear your "tightness" and you will be dialing up your desires in the etherial universe, and probably in your real life!

HARMONY – Vertical

Sometimes it's great to go "out-of-time" and just tell musicians to play a certain chord until cued to the next chord, this is truly seeing HARMONY AS VERTICAL. It's similar to how an enlightened Buddhist would say there is ONLY THE NOW. Rhythm goes along horizontally just as time does, but Harmony is in the immediate this second, totally vertical, unlimited height; that's a revelatory technique and it definitely ties in to this area of study. Of course **all pitches are frequency** just like rhythms and timing.

For some people the way to describe notes is the do-re-mi-fa-so-la-ti system. Fa = the 4th, so the 5th, la the 6th, etc..

Letter Names Of Notes On Instruments

Piano and Keyboards

All keyboards have the same general layout. The middle C on the piano is C3. You should always know how to find the letter notes quickly on keyboards.

Some people put the letter names on every key of their keyboard.

Cut out little As, Bs, Cs and so on. Let students lick the back and put them on keyboards.

There are little sheets you can slide carefully behind the black notes of your keyboard that show all the letter names of the notes. Whatever helps you know the letters is good.

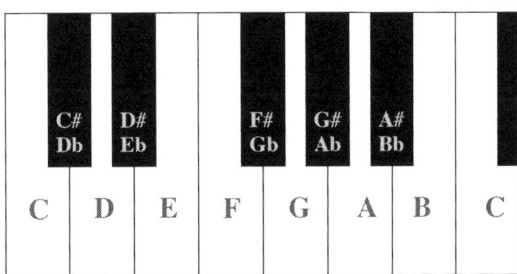

Once you remember them, it's easy. All keyboards will have sets of 2 black notes, then three black notes. Just below the 2 black notes is the note "C." The note between the 2 black notes is "D." The next note is "E," and you can see how the system works, going up to "G" and then starting with "A" again.

Here's a trick you can use. Since you need to "See sharp!" what note is what, quickly spot the 2 black notes. The lowest one is C#! There is no C flat, you want to see sharp!

Note Letter Names on **String** Instruments

Guitar

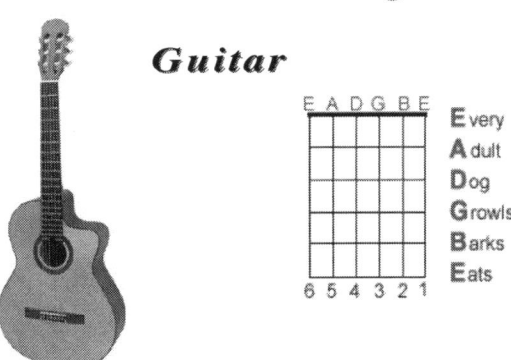

The bottom and top strings of a guitar are the note E. The notes of guitars are a fourth apart – E to A is a forth, A to D a fourth, etc. The only different one is G to B which is a 3rd. See that on the keyboard. Notice how many ½ steps it is between E and A. The notes of the guitar are E2 A2 D3 G3 B3 E4. Bass guitar is all fourths E0 A1 D1 G1.

On most guitars you can easily see where to put your finger to be a fourth above, notice that violins don't have those lines (called **frets**) to help! These musicians know instinctually where to put their fingers to get a fourth above.

You can put your finger down on the 7th fret of a guitar and get the fifth above. Another technique, that doesn't even require the frets **but is maybe even more exact** is this:

 **Just where the 7th fret is, hold your finger on the string to get the harmonic – notice it is exactly an octave and a fifth above! This is called an overtone.**

String Instrument Family

While guitars are said to be in fourths, violins are in fifths: Violin is G2 D3 A4 E4, viola C2 G2 D3 A4. cello is C1 G1 D2 A3.

 **Whatever instruments are in the classroom, play a C on them**

Whatever instruments are in the classroom, play a D on them

 **Have students when they go home write down what notes are on the instruments at home**

double bass   cello   viola   violin

How to Find the Notes for a Song

Whether or not it is a song or just music in your head, it is a great thing to find it on your instrument, and then write it down for the future.

Keep it in your head, and go to your instrument and find the first note. Write the letter name of the note down. Continue finding the notes of the song and writing down the letters. This is a great start at scoring!

Notes that are shorter you can write closer to each other, so that Beethoven's Fifth would look like:

Eb Eb Eb C---   D D D B---   Eb Eb Eb C G G G Eb C C C G

And so on. Make whatever other notes help you remember what you are hearing, they always help!

If you can, use the information below and put the notes on musical staffs, or ask a friend to do it for you.

World Music Compilation 8

How to Teach Yourself to Read Short Music Scores

Using the picture of the piano keyboard with the lines of the musical staffs and middle C that is on page 13 (ahead 5 pages) and looking at a short score you want to learn, just start finding the notes on the staff one note at a time.

It is especially good if the song is "in your ear," and you remember it well enough that you will know when you play a wrong note.

Take your time and find the first few notes from the score on the piano, and play them while reassuring yourself that they are the right notes to the song.

You may want to play as much as you can play on the instrument, and then sing the rest. A big part of playing on instruments is visualizing the music in your head. In one sense the instrument is just an extension of you – like a car or screwdriver or spoon.

Be patient and once you have part of the song in your head, keep repeating it so that you won't forget it.

Nowadays with everyone having so many gadgets, you can probably find a phone, laptop, walkman tape recorder or something to let you record yourself playing what you have learned. This is good 1) to hear it and get ideas to improve it, and 2) so that if you can't practice for a little while you can listen and remember exactly what you have achieved!

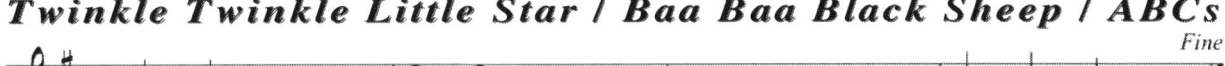

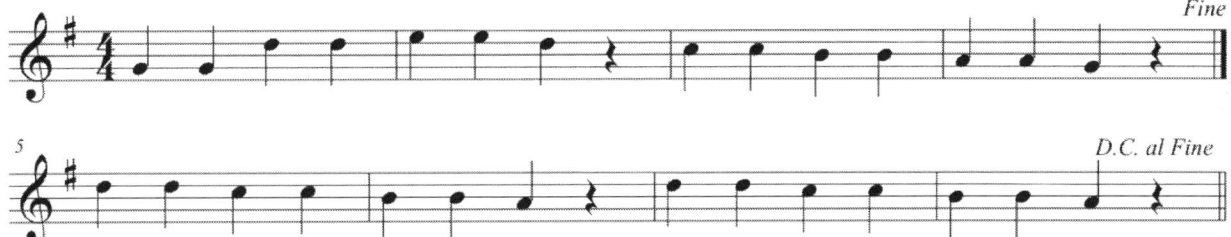

Make up inspirational songs like: *Twinkle twinkle shining star, when you practice you go far. As you practice every night, you are happy, playing right…* Practice scoring by writing out the songs Baa Baa Black Sheep & the ABCs.

Intervals Between Notes

Between any two notes is call an interval. Between B and C is a semitone or half step.

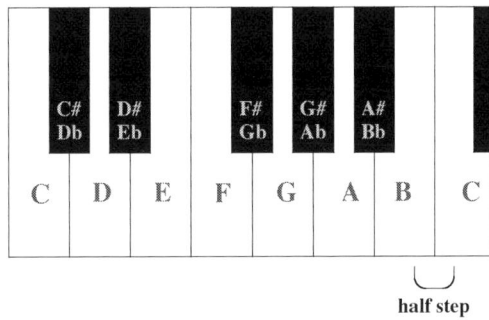

Between C and D is a whole step, whole tone or whole note.

World Music Compilation 9

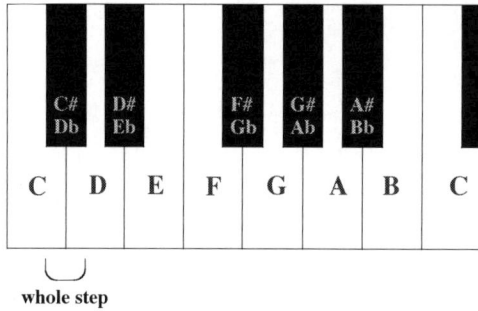

A half step is called a "Diminished 2nd." A whole step is called a "Perfect 2nd."

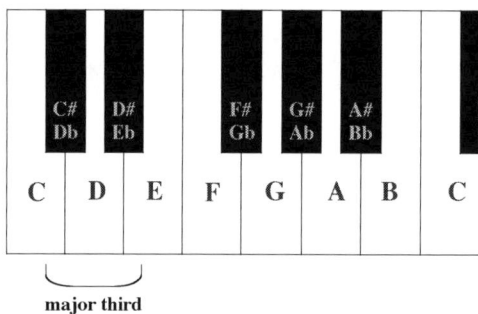

Thirds, from A to C or from C to E are called differently. They are called Major and Minor.

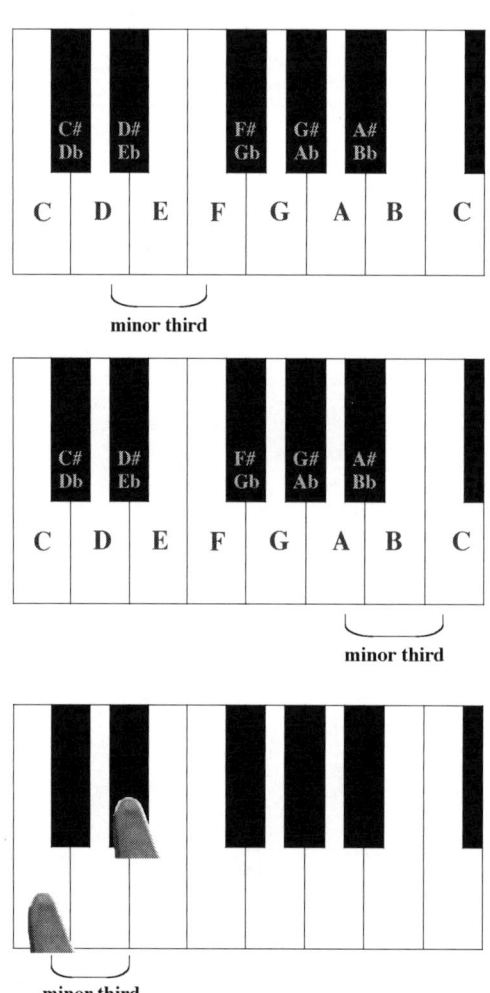

Each interval has specific terms to describe if it is slightly less or slightly more.

Basic Intervals on the Treble Clef

Table of Intervals & numbers of Semitones & Whole Tones

Interval	Semitones	Whole Tones
Diminished 2nd	1	0
Perfect 2nd	2	1
Augmented 2nd & Minor 3rd	3	1 ½
Major 3rd	4	2
Perfect 4th	5	2 ½
Augmented 4th & Diminished 5th	6	3
Perfect 5th	7	3 ½
Augmented 5th & Minor 6th	8	4
Major 6th	9	4 ½
Minor 7th	10	5
Major 7th	11	5 ½
Perfect Octave	12	6

A 9th, though useful, is simply reduced to being a 2nd. The 10th is simply the 3rd, the 11th the fourth, and so on. For the sake of Harmony, the intervals don't really matter what octave they are in. For example: Any octave of C and any octave of E and any octave of G is always considered the 1-3-5 of a C Major chord, completely regardless of octaves.

For any note you need to know how to find the note above or below it, using ALL of the intervals in the table above. Example: from G, find the note a perfect 5th above, then a perfect 5th below.

It can not be overstressed how useful it is for those who wish to know music to be able to find any interval from any note, and also the reverse, determine what interval any note is from any other.

The common practice is: if someone asks for an interval, and doesn't specify diminished, perfect, augmented, major or minor, then it will be the most common one – perfect and major. In other words "give me a 6th" means give me a major 6th.

 Someone play a random note. Someone else find a third above it. Someone else, a fifth above it.

Some intervals are associated with certain things. The Operator tone on the phone is the diminished 5th of E and Bb. Ambulances usually have this interval. Door chimes are usually a major chord, similar to the three notes mentioned above though often in another order. Show Sol-Mi-Do.

This example is from an old reference: Have 3 people sing the word "Hello!" and hold it, singing the Do-Mi-So of a major chord and hold it. I always want to add the minor 7th above (from an old Three Stooges show).

Intervals going up and down

Intervals going up are the exact inverse of the interval coming down. They add up to nine: Up a 2nd is down a 7th. Up a 3rd is down a 6th. Up a 4th is down a 5th. Up a 5th is down a 4th, Up a 6th is down a 3rd. Up a 7th is down a 2nd.

One way to remember intervals is to come up with a song for every interval, so that you can think of that song, or play it, and then you can remember the interval.

Play an octave, ask students what song it makes them think of. Let them sing it if they like.

Intervals Add Up To Chords

The major chord is composed of a major third and a minor third. The minor chord is a minor chord and a major third. The top and bottom notes of these chords are a perfect fifth. The diminished (C°) chord is made of two minor thirds and the distance from the top to the bottom note is a diminished (flat) fifth.

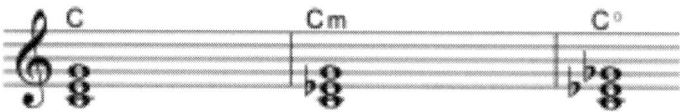

All chords are made up of intervals.

Can you think up other ways to add intervals together and get chords? Share them!

Hint: a 6th is also a 3rd… If you start on the note G and go up a 6th, then do it again, what chord is that?

Ranges and Transpositions

Ranges of Soprano, Alto, Tenor and Bass (S-A-T-B)

These change depending on the singers capabilities, but this is a good general rule.

Piano Range, Keyboard with Staff lines and ledger lines

The piano has 88 keys, and let's see what the exact range is. Each octave (from C to C) has 12 steps. 88 is 7*12 (84) plus 4, so four more than 7 octaves. The lowest note is "A" technically notated: "A0." It is interesting that it's frequency, in times per second that it vibrates, is the same as the low of our alternating current, AC voltage is 55 to 60 Hz, Hertz, times per second. The A above that one is A1, 110hz, A2 is 220hz, A3 is middle A, 440. The piano goes up to A7 and then the C above that, so the piano keyboard we know goes from A0 to C7.

See that above C3, middle C, are the 5 lines of the treble clef. The letters E G B D F = **Every Good Boy Does Fine**. The bass clef G B D F A = **Good Boy Does Fine Always**.

Instrument Ranges & Transposing for them

C Piccolo written: D3 – G♭5 actually: D4 - G♭6

C Flute: C3 – C6

Oboe: B♭3 – F5

English Horn written: B3 – F5 actually: E2 - B♭5

Bassoon: B♭1 - B♭4

Contra-Bassoon written: B♭0 - E♭2

B♭ Clarinet written: E2 – G5 actually: D2 – F5

B♭ Clarinet (French system, most common) written: E2 – G5 actually D1 – F4

B♭ Clarinet (German system) written: E1 – G4 actually: D1 – F4

B♭ Trumpet written: F#2 – D5 actually E2 – C5

French Horn written: C2 – C5 actually F1 – F4

Tenor Trombone: E1 - B♭4

Bass Trombone: B♭1 – F3

Bass Tuba: E0 - B♭3

Violin: G2 – C6

Viola: C2 – E5

Cello: C1 – E5

String Bass written: E1 – G3 actually: E0 – G2

B♭ Soprano Sax written: B♭3 – F5 actually: A♭3 - E♭5

E♭ Alto Sax written: B♭3 – F5 actually: D♭2 - A♭5

B♭ Tenor Sax written: B♭3 – F5 actually: A♭2 - E♭4

E♭ Baritone Sax written: B♭3 – F5 actually: D♭1 - A♭4

B♭ Bass Sax written B♭3 – F5 actually A♭1 - E♭3

The Circle of Fifths

Circle of Fifths Graphic

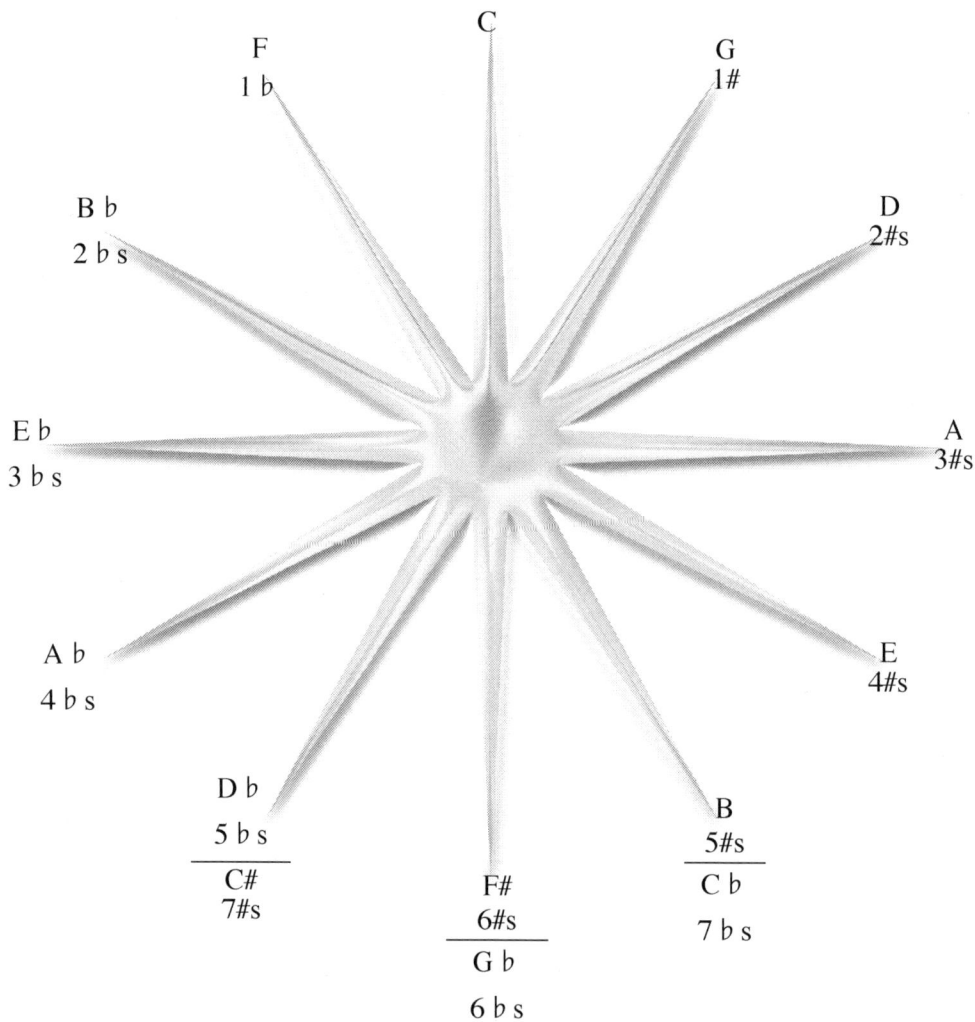

D♭ is the same as C#, it is said "ENHARMONICALLY" they are the same. Also F# = G♭ and B = C♭.

Some people would say that keys with flats are for horns, horns are usually in B♭ or E♭. Guitars, and the string music family are generally in E or A, songs written on them will be in these keys, so those instruments and their songs are in sharp keys.

A song can be in any key though. From the above you can see there is a system to how many sharps and flats a key has. For each additional sharp or flat you go a fifth – 7 half steps away – up for sharps and down for flats.

Circle of Fifths on the Keyboard

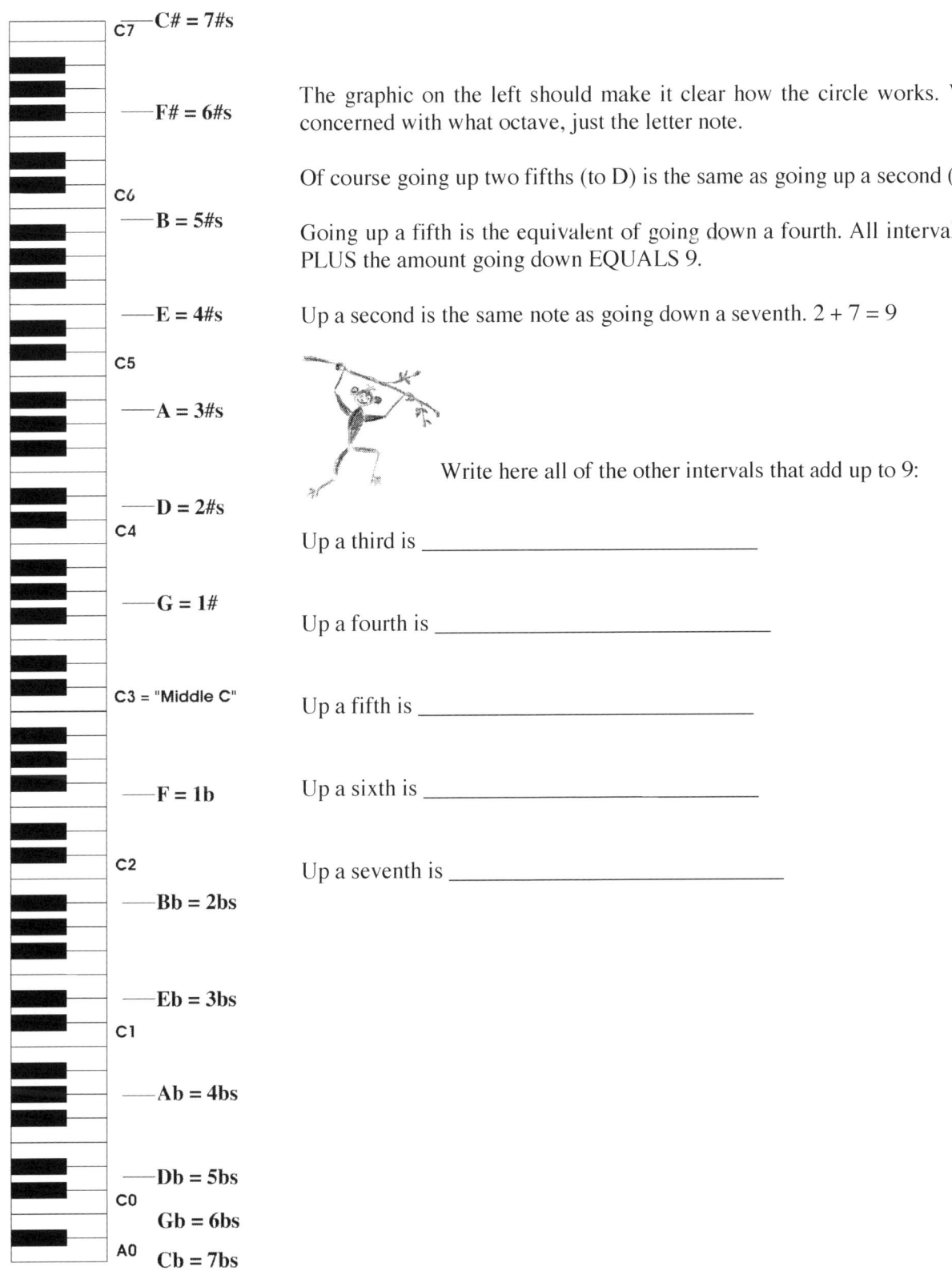

The graphic on the left should make it clear how the circle works. We are not concerned with what octave, just the letter note.

Of course going up two fifths (to D) is the same as going up a second (to D).

Going up a fifth is the equivalent of going down a fourth. All intervals going up PLUS the amount going down EQUALS 9.

Up a second is the same note as going down a seventh. 2 + 7 = 9

Write here all of the other intervals that add up to 9:

Up a third is _____

Up a fourth is _____

Up a fifth is _____

Up a sixth is _____

Up a seventh is _____

World Music Compilation 15

Key Signatures

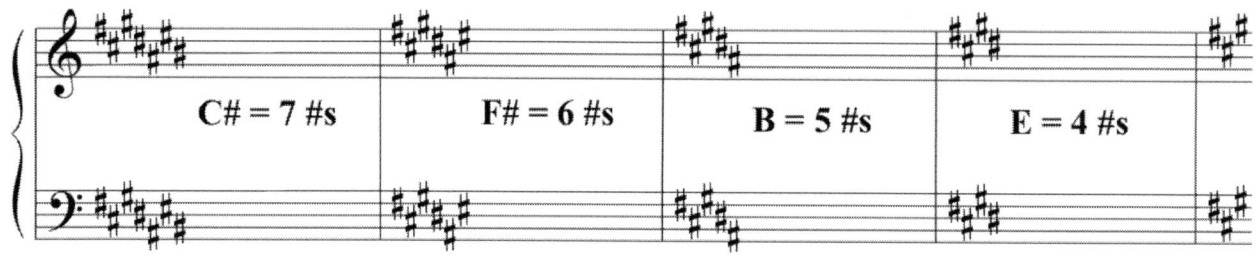
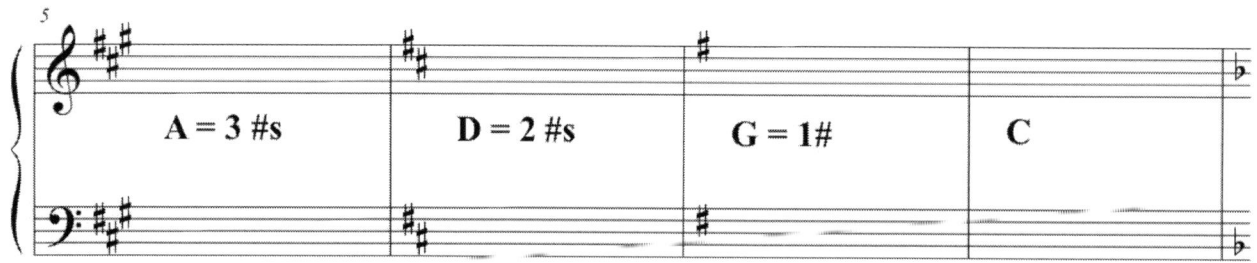
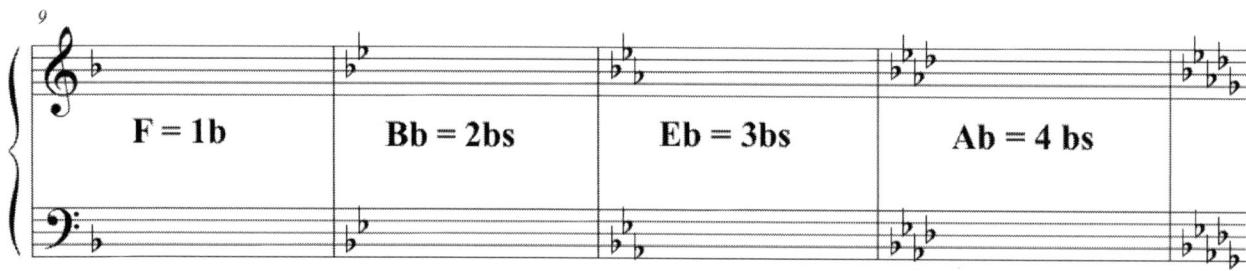
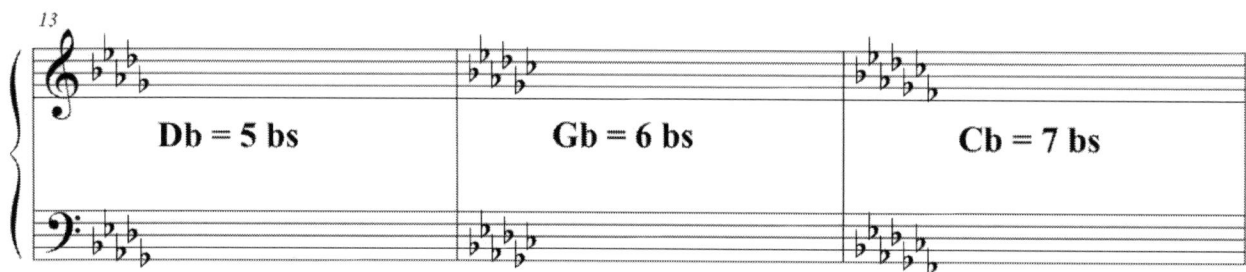

Minor Key Signatures

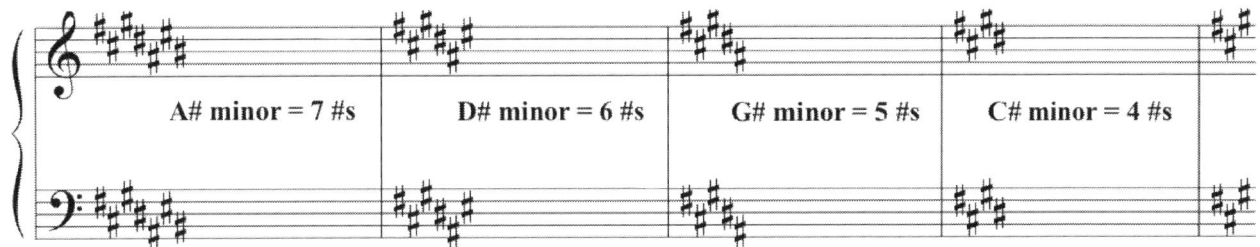
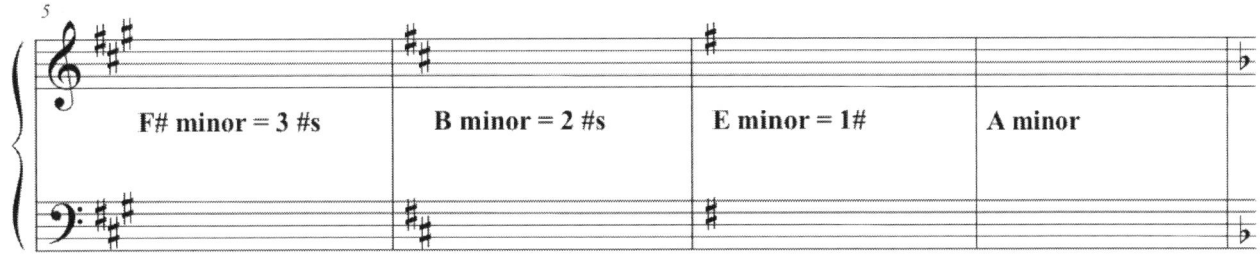
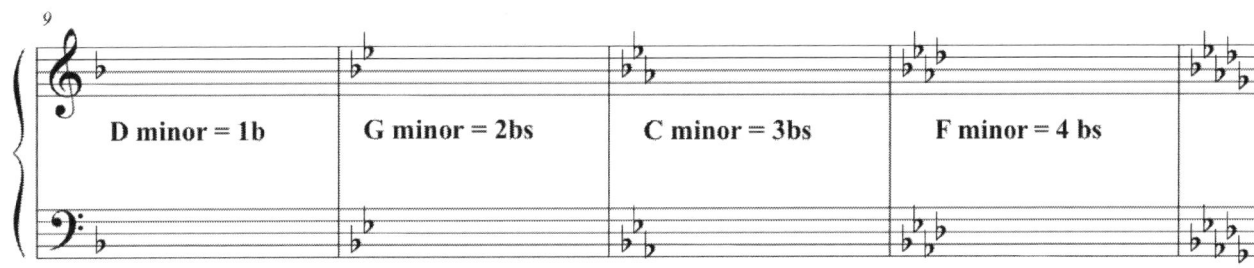
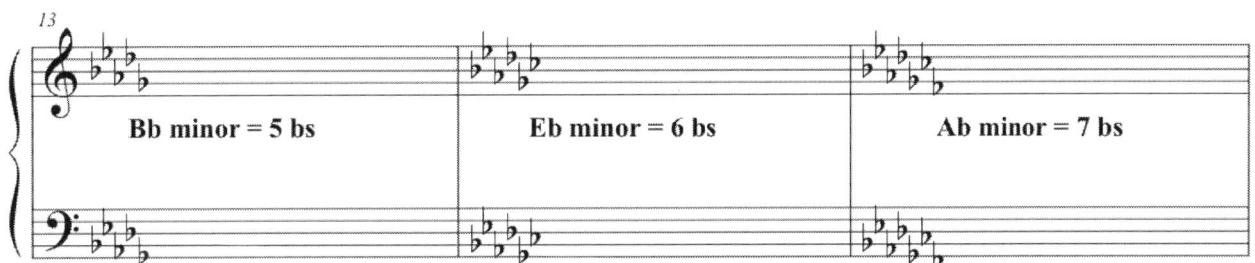

A double flat simply looks like two flat symbols like this:

A double sharp is a funny kind of x and looks like this:

Harmonics

The Harmonic Series

Root, A open string = 110 hz, hertz, times per second

1st Overtone, an octave above, A = 220 hz

2nd Overtone is a 5th above, E = 330 hz.

Can you guess what the note, and frequency of the **3rd overtone** is? The hint is this: You divide the string into 4 parts.

Did you guess it yet? Well, the frequency is 440, that should tell you that like halving the open string (110) gives us an octave above, (220), halving the half, or dividing it into equal quarters gives us the next overtone, the next octave of A, and in this case the most common note: "La equals 440!" All instruments tune to.

Here is the **harmonic system**, also called the **overtone series**, on a piano keyboard, starting on the note 'C,' and you will see where the **major chord** comes from:

* ROOT NOTE = C1
* FIRST OVERTONE = C2
* SECOND OVERTONE = G2
* THIRD OVERTONE = C3
* FOURTH OVERTONE = E3
* FIFTH OVERTONE = G3
* SIXTH OVERTONE = A3

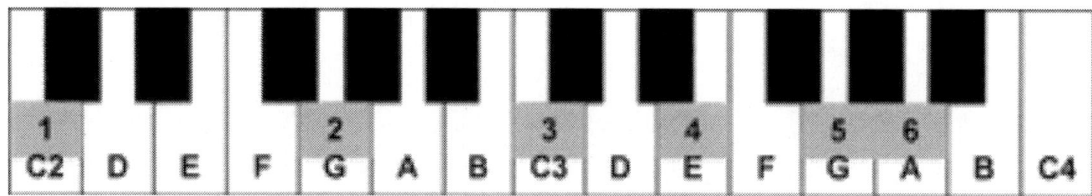

The Science of Harmonics

Tuning with harmonics / overtones

Reviewing regular fretted tuning:
5th fret of E is A. 5th fret of A is D. 5th fret of D is G. 4th fret of G is B. 5th fret of B is E.

From the above you know where the 5th fret is (or would be). Also you must know where the 7th fret is (or would be) – it gives you the perfect 5th if you hold it down OR get the harmonic, the overtone.

When you have string 1 tuned: Using overtones, tune string 2 7th fret to string 1 5th fret. Next tune string 3 7th fret to string 2 5th fret. Next tune string 4 7th fret to string 3 5th fret. Next tune string 5 open to string 1 7th fret. Finally tune string 6 open to string 2 7th fret.

Playing "Revile" with harmonic overtones

The song that wakes the troops up, "Revile," is made up of the same notes as the harmonic series we are describing. The first three notes are (overtones of) 7th fret, 5th fret, 4th fret. Later there is one higher note, 3rd fret.

Sine and Square waves, the mouth as a filter

When you make the "oo" sound with your mouth, that is a pure sine wave, as we imagine it. The "ee" sound is the square wave, yes, it looks square. As you open your mouth from "oo" to "ee," if you go slowly, you will hear the overtones / harmonics show up. First the octave, then the 5th above that, just like the keyboard graphic just above.

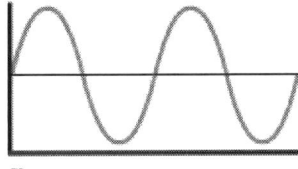
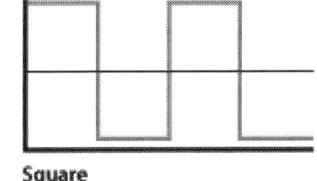

The 'naturally occurring' overtones help to see how notes are added up to create chords. A chord is a series of notes on top of each other, generally using a **1 - 3 - 5 - 7 - 9** etc.. system.

Greek Modes or Scales

Johann Wolfgang von Goethe said "Architecture is frozen music." Columns were **Doric**, then **Ionic**, then **Corinthian** (as Rick Steves the travel guide says, each era added a syllable ☺). Our music modes system is different but similar. Yes, these were modes of music used even in Greek times. Some names are different.

Greek Mode	Roman Letter	Solfege	White Notes	Also Known As	Scale Degree	Quality
Ionian	I	Do	C to C	Major Scale	Tonic	Major
Dorian	ii	Re	D to D	Dorian Minor	Supertonic	Minor
Phrygian	iii	Mi	E to E	*Phrygian Scale*	Mediant	Minor
Lydian	IV	Fa	F to F	Lydian Major	Subdominant	Major
Mixolydian	V	So	G to G	Dominant Scale	Dominant	Dominant
Aolean	vi	La	A to A	Natural Minor	Submediant	Minor
Locrean	vii	Ti (Si)	B to B	*Locrean Scale*	Leading Note	Diminished

The following scale doesn't fit into the above list, for one thing it has the sharp 2nd or *augmented* 2nd interval.

Harmonic Minor Dominant – *(Flamenco / Middle Eastern / Phrygian Dominant / Freygish)*

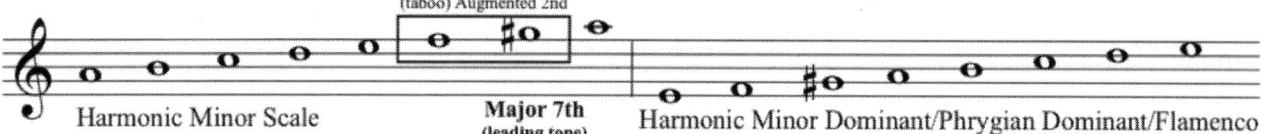

This scale is tons of fun! You'll sound like a Genie, or Andalusian Gypsy King! Play around with it!!

Make a fun game of who knows the song!

This song is a perfect example of the Middle Eastern / Harmonic Minor Dominant scale. Do you recognize it? It is the best example of this scale ever, and truly a beautiful, fun song.

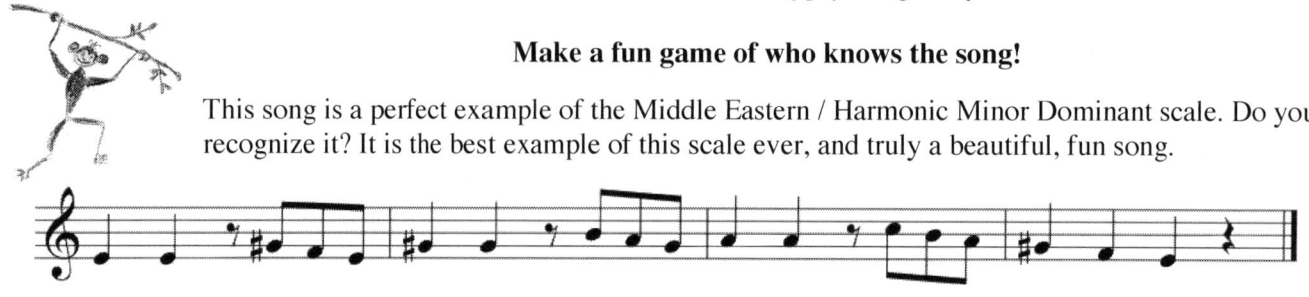

The following is a form figure that goes around a circle of fifths (called a *sequence*) in an interesting way. Sure it looks complicated with all the chords completely spelled out, but you'll see that it is not really that difficult to play. In the title notice the Re=D, sol=G, mi=E, la=A, fa=F and ti=Bb. The *8vb* with the dashed line means play it an octave lower. The Ped. and star symbols mean sustain pedal and release. They look like pretty flowers ☺.

This can be a building block for a song, or improvisation, or ensemble work (fun playing together). Enjoy it!

Resolmilafatimila
Form Figure No. 1

Slowly with feeling

Teo Vincent IV
(c) 2011

Spelled out: The 1st 4 notes up and down is a D minor 9, the next 4 is a G 13 over D, the next 4 an E minor 7 with a flat 5th and flat 9th, the next 4 an A 7 with a sharp 5th and flat 9th over E, the next a F Major 9, the next a Bb Major 9 over F, the next 4 an E minor 7 with a flat 5th, the next 4 an A 7 with a sharp 5th and flat 9th over E, then D minor 9 again (you see that **m**inor is lower case, **M**ajor and **S**eventh are uppercase). How nice that playing these simple 18 bars above, all the chords you'll know. ☺ Try this intro: start by repeating bars 9-12 (F & Bb chords), then play 13-16, then start at the beginning.

The song is *modal*, in a mode. The "Do" is C Dominant (the Bb), Mixolydian, not Ionian. Funny how it sounds like: "He's in a mood, his resolution is odd." It is as if music is the true understanding of moods (*they are modes?*).

World Music Mastery, Building Blocks for Playing With Anyone!

Start with just the left hand, soon you will see and know how a chord is 1-3-5 and how to make the common ones.

* Quarter tied to eighth note is more correct. ** Bass can be 1-3-5 as in bar 1 or 1-5-1 as in bar 15.

Notice the ROMAN NUMBERS for each chord. Lower case are minor. A "Progression" is a set of chords. You should be able to play I-IV-V in any key, as in these examples. Also i-iv-V=minor. Continue on your own up chromatic as the last three staves/staffs here do. The next is iv-i-V-i in C minor, then C# minor. Notice with these that go iv-i-V-I, f you start on the 4th bar it is i-iv-i-V! Songs can shift like this in the middle! Learn every key.

Common Chords

Triads, chords that are 1 – 3 – 5

Here are the common chords on the treble clef of the musical staff, in C:

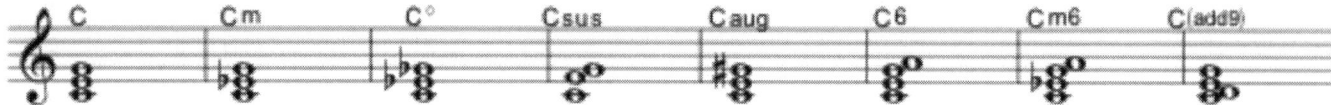

On piano keyboard:

C or C Major (in classical harmony "C+") = C – E – G.

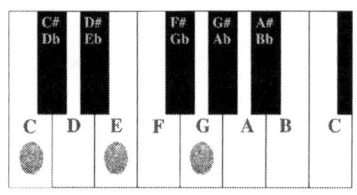

(Try major chords in circles like C, F, Bb, Eb, Ab, Db, Gb, B, E, A, D, G, C whala! Great practice!)

C minor or Cm or C- = C – Eb – G

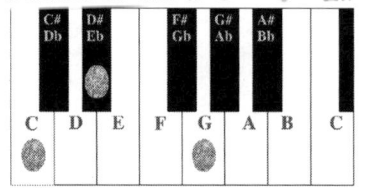

C diminished or C dim or C° = C - Eb - Gb

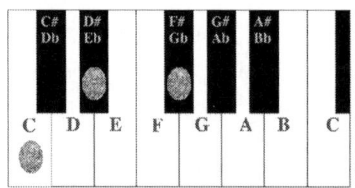

C Suspended or C sus = C - F - G

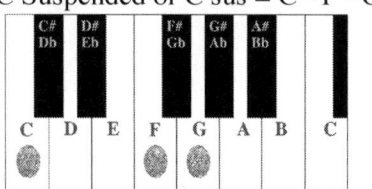

C Augmented or C aug or C+ = C - E - G#

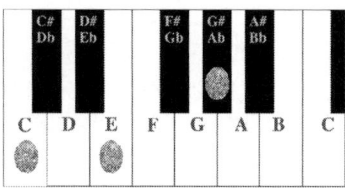

Seventh Chords 1 – 3 – 5 – 7

Notice: if someone calls out "**F Seven**" it is the *Dominant Seventh* chord that is they mean, not the *Major Seventh* chord – unlike how with Triad chords, *Triads*, above, if someone calls out "F!" or "F Chord!" they mean F Major. With 7ths you have to specify if you want a Major Seventh. The default, if you just see the letter and number, is a dominant 7th chord, which has a major third and a minor or flat 7th.

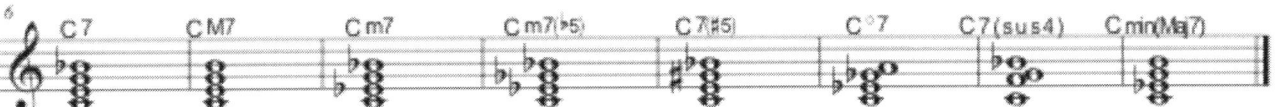

C Seven or C Seventh or C Dominant or C Dominant 7th or C7 = C - E - G - Bb

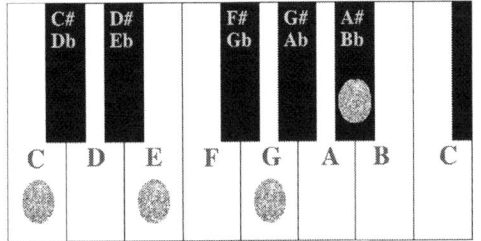

C Major 7th or CM7 or CΔ or CMaj7 = C - E - G - B

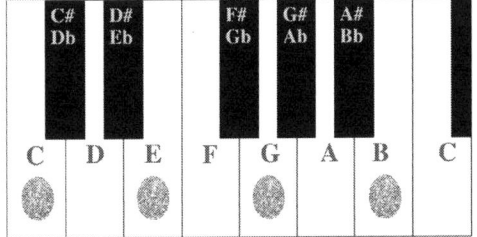

C minor 7th or C min 7 or Cm7 or C-7 = C - Eb - G - Bb

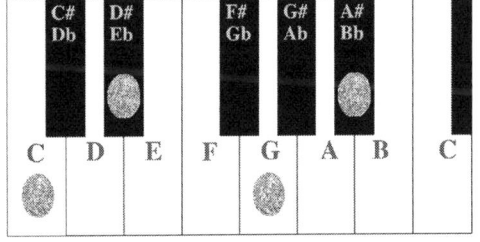

C Half Diminished or C minor diminished 7 or Cm7(b5) or Cø7 = C - Eb - Gb - Bb

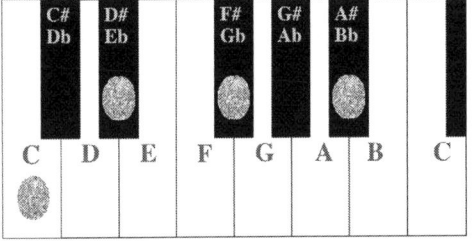

C Fully Diminished or C Diminished 7 or C°7 = C - Eb - Gb - A

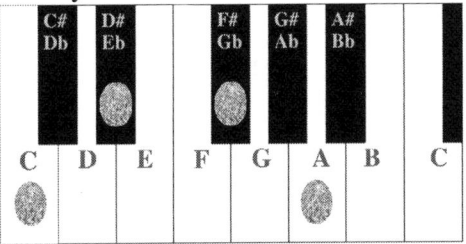

C Seven Suspended or C Seven Sus or C Seventh Suspended or C Seventh Sus or C7sus = C - F - G - Bb

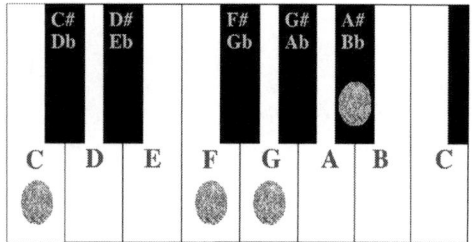

 **In the space next to the keyboard graphics above, write out each interval.** For example: C to F = perfect fourth. F to G = perfect 2nd. G to Bb = Minor Third.

You can additionally do all the other intervals, such as C to Bb, C to G and F to Bb.

One of the best exercises you can ever do is to go around the circle of fifths and at the same time practice ii-V-I or 2-5-1. A great way is like: Am D7 GM " Gm C7 FM " Fm Bb7 EbM " Ebm Ab7 DbM " Dbm Gb7 BM " Bm E7 AM " Am D7 GM etc.. First just do one hand, then when you feel you understand the system put the roots in the left hand. This is truly one of the best exercises you can do. Here are some good basic 7th chords from the affirmation song "My Successes Are Here" later in this book:

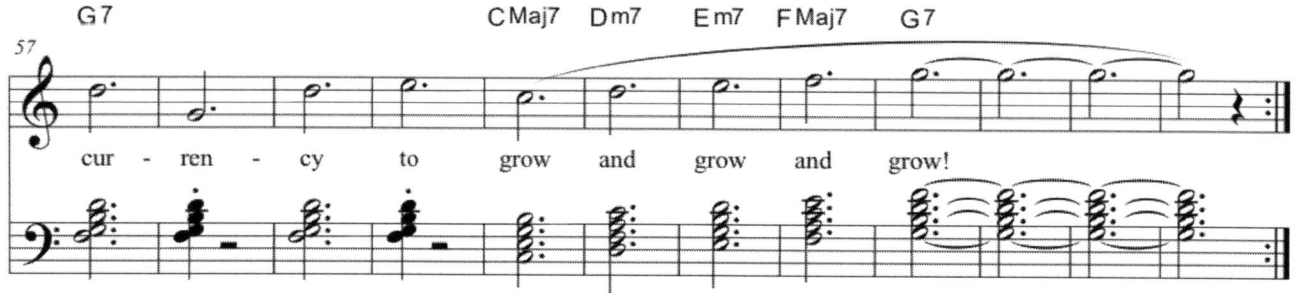

In this section from Johan Sebastian Bach's Prelude #1 you see the G7(sus) to G7 is noted below (in *figured bass* style) as **V 7/4-------3**. Try playing the G7sus4 and then G7 to see what Bach is showing us here.

Latin Piano (Montuno) 101: "La Bamba" C I-IV-V-IV major and minor (with I-ii-V-ii variation) *learn in all keys*

Heuristic Music Learning

Here our intention is to teach you how to learn music by yourself, starting with being able to write down melodies you hear or know, then writing down the chord progression so that accompanists can play it too.

heuristic
As an adjective, heuristic (pronounced hyu-RIS-tik and from the Greek "heuriskein" meaning "to discover") pertains to the process of gaining knowledge or some desired result by intelligent guesswork rather than by following some pre-established formula. - *http://WhatIs.com*

We at Givnology with our Educational and Media Technologies look at what makes a superior trainer, helping students know how to learn by themselves. Encourage them to bring in whatever manuals or instructions they have, and show them ways to utilize the resources that they already have to their optimum. This would mean showing them sections of instructions they should take care to learn thoroughly, or sections of reference materials that they should keep handy and use frequently. In addition supply students with lists of shortcuts, and techniques to make step-by-step instructions for themselves or others.

In music, encouraging students to learn by themselves is a vastly different task, but has many of the same strategies. What makes it different is the extent to which people should find out how to find the music within, the traditional songs of their cultures, or even other people's cultures that they admire and want to honor (if appropriate).

Unlike other learning, there are things that one who wants to learn music on their own should do that are completely personal and have *everything* to do with their particular backgrounds and inclinations. The greatest advantage of learning music on one's own, being one's own teacher, is that one can study exactly what one wants to study!

If your are a Beethoven-head, you can immerse yourself endlessly in Ludwig's thoughts, emotions, stories and music. If you want to study the traditional music of your ancestors, you can dig deeply into it without having to be concerned with anything else.

Firstly, like any learning, prepare with plenty of paper, pens – erasables are great! Mechanical pencils are awesome, yellow highlighters and stick-it pads to use as notes and bookmarks so that your books are kept in tip-top shape while having many color-coded easy to find tabs with just-what-you-want, just-when-you-want-it! In addition, walkmans or small tape recorders are very inexpensive nowadays, we suggest having one or two so that you can sing or play any idea into it without having to go to a recording studio – to make sure you don't lose that genius amazing inspiration that came to you at 2AM. **Make sure to have plenty of supplies.**

Always tell music students to learn enough to be able to write down basic music phrases on a musical staff. This only requires knowing the pitches, where the notes are vertically on the staff, and note values: whole notes, half, quarter notes, sixteenth and so on, and rests. All these things are very easy to get a basic grasp on.

The easiest way would be to have a friend help you write down a melody that you love. By seeing how the sounds and lengths translate into circles with various flags, rests between and put between bar lines, you will make the connection between what you know as music and how it looks on paper.

You can also find a score of a song you know well. When you can look at the score and see the same sounds that you know, you will have bridged the skills you already have over to this new task: knowing what written music looks like.

Once you can do the basics of writing a melody on a staff, which is no small accomplishment, you can basically start to analyze music on your own. The next step is to understand what keys or chords should be used underneath the melody that you have written.

Our goal here is that you can score music for your self and for others to collaborate or to help you play it better or together, in an ensemble. If you are to play with a solo instrument like a flute, simply writing the melody out is enough. If you want to play with accompaniment such as guitar, piano, accordion, ukulele or keyboard, etc., you will need to know what a chord progression is, and what the common ones are. Sometimes you will use a standard set of chords – whether or not the song originally had them! Common chord progressions are:

I – IV – V – I or "1-4-5." This is the most common in all songs! Some songs have less chord and may stay in I for most of the song, maybe going to V for a climactic type of finale, then back to I. Others may go I to IV, to ii, to VI, to VIb (flat six) to V to I or wherever it wants! Again, the above suggestion is best: have someone show you the chord chart for a song you like or know well. See how the root moves here and there, and see how you could sometimes use a different chord structure for the same song!

Be A Useful Member Of Your Music Projects

You should always have a SONG LIST / KEY LIST / CHEAT SHEET for the project or group's songs. If you are blessed enough to keep it all in your head, fine. What about when your favorite other musician want's the same overview of CHORDS, STYLES, ARTISTS, and LYRIC SHEETS that you've prepared for yourself? **Make these lists available to others too** and the musical organization you do will come back to you.

You should also be extremely reliable, because musicians have a bad reputation for reliability that you should help overcome. Call people back, and promptly, so that they can know what's going on, if they can use you in their project.

Go over your material A LOT!!! It is always obvious at a session or rehearsal who has been doing their woodshedding (rehearsing on their own). That's the sort of negative way to look at this, let's look at the positives: The more you practice all the material, and other similar material, and work with other members on it, the more latitude you'll have in the session! If you've found another song in the same style that your project is working on and it really helps you get into the feel and vibe of the style, have the cats warm up on that song. It might make the difference between people doing the least that they can and a group collaborative learning and uplifting experience! Once you've done your homework, there is no reason you can't share all the tricks and techniques you've found with your co-artists.

So get a walkman tape deck (or 5) and be able to run over the material 24-7. If someone else in the project says they don't have time for that, make them a tape and loan them a walkman. You might just save the musical project, and you'll have others to learn with together. Making others in the project notes, tapes, charts and such really helps you all bond and they'll be sharing their chops with you too!

Fine Playing on Keyboard

There are many people who would never believe you can learn piano playing on an electric keyboard. They might be right! At the same time, they are extremely handy, and with more and more pluses and benefits than ever before like *They never need tuning, You can instantly play in any key, You can take them anywhere!*

Children have become addicted to their techno-boxes. Get them addicted to Casio and Yamaha, off of Nintendo and Game-Boy. A financially strapped music budget can still afford these and not cancel classes! People can be asked to donate old keyboards as they get better ones.

If you are brand new to music, or thinking of starting playing again, there are many things you can do with inexpensive electronic keyboards. Considering their extremely low cost, **you can get started right away.** It is not uncommon for people to loan you (or even just give you) a keyboard. The range in prices is so big, and there are so many features and options you should know about.

First, let us overview what you can do on **Keyboard vs. Piano:**

	Learn Chords	Fingering of Scales	Learn Songs	Easy Play Organ	Play with Sensitivity	Play Dynamics	Extreme Dynamics	Stays in Tune	Requires Electricity	Take Anywhere
Keyboard	Y	Y	Y	Y	?	?	N	Y	Y	Y
Piano	Y	Y	Y	N	Y	Y	Y	N	N	N

There are many other things Keyboards can do such as: easily change to another key (transpose), record MIDI files (".mid" are very small files you can send easily to people, and are easily made into phone ring-tones)

1) Velocity Sensitivity = you push harder, it is louder. Only very inexpensive keyboards are not velocity sensitive. In Classical music you might see *pppp* = very *pianissimo*, very quiet, *pp* = quiet. All the way to *ffff* = *fortissimo*, very loud. You can not really do this on a keyboard (not a cheap one anyway).

2) 16 not polyphonic = usually enough, unless you have to hold down a 5 note chord, sustain, and play 4 or more octaves of it (the top 4 notes won't sound, or the bottom 4 will stop being sustained). For beginners even 8 note polyphony is OK – but on some keyboards some nice sounds (called tones) require doubling! To get a nice piano tone the 8 note polyphony becomes 4, too low.

3) Speakers or Amplifier. Most have speakers. Some people get a **Controller** (or master) keyboard that has nice action & playability, then a separate sound unit. It is easy enough to plug a MIDI cable in the MIDI out of the controller and the MIDI in of the sound unit (sometimes called slave). By default all MIDI operates on channel 1, and piano is the default sound. This option is nice because you can get an inexpensive sound unit like a Yamaha PSR for $200 or so, then an expensive controller like the M-Audio which is weighted, 88 keys with many controls very easy to get to.

4) 61 keys = enough to learn the basic repertoire. Also enough to practice your scales. This is the standard 5 octave keyboard that is very inexpensive. You can usually switch octave and have it play as low as a real piano, or as high. Get 2 and you have more notes than a piano!

5) Sustain pedal = really required to sound reasonable at all on a keyboard. In the awful case that you forget one, you can stick a clothespin in the sustain jack and have all notes sustain all the time which at least is better than the lame sound with no sustain at all! Some people would just use a sustaining tone like church organ, but the best idea is keep an extra sustain pedal – it really will save you!

What you *CAN* learn on keyboards:

Fur Elise, Mozart Menuet, Bach Prelude #1, Satie Gymnopedies, Chopin A Major Prelude, Scales, Fingerings, Common Chords, etc..

You can learn much of the general knowledge about music, and keyboards from a keyboard. The name of the instrument: "Piano" actually means the word "soft." Going back in time to the evolution of the piano of today, the first ancestor was called the "Piano y Forte." This is because of it's amazing ability to get very very quiet, and also very very loud.

This exact difference in volume is one of the main things you can not really do on keyboards. It takes a very delicate touch, and even though keyboards might cost in the 10s of thousands, some pianos cost $100,000 or more!

The goal is to be expressive. Emotional. Sensitive. Play with feeling!

There have always been more and less expressive pianists. To be a real fine classical pianist, you will play parts of the song so quiet it is barely audible and some people will have to turn up their stereos, then some parts jump out so loud that people will be leaping to the volume knob to turn it back down. This is music with full dynamics – very loud to very soft.

This ties in with another very important part of fine playing: phrasing. Each part should flow as if it was being sung. Try singing along with yourself while playing the part, it really helps. Overdo the quiet and loud parts.

Some pieces of some songs require brute force, jarring pounding and generally sounding like a mean person. Other songs, or parts of songs, can sound as delicate as a butterfly. Knowing how to express this vast range of emotions and moods is playing expressively.

Chopin was called "The poet of the piano." Poetics is the art of truly fine piano playing. He composed exclusively for the piano, except for a handful of pieces. He truly mastered an expressive, sensitive and emotion-conveying technique that few others ever came close to, though his close friend Franz Liszt came close. They wrote Etudes (that word simply means studies in French) to each other.

Can you be *POETIC* on a keyboard? Likely not. With everything we are telling you here, you can improve your piano poetics, and maybe sound OK. Still, when you get to a real piano you need to focus on the things you can't learn at all on a keyboard.

FINE PLAYING *techniques when you have access to a real piano:*

Extreme staccato (short punched sound) like Schumann's "Wild Horses" or peppy songs like Marches.

Dynamics (pianissimo and forte) like in Beethoven's Fur Elise's 3rd and 4th sections or other moody pieces.

Things that make the smaller fingers work out hard. Practice major 9ths in both hands, arpeggiate them, go up and down the keyboard until your fingers feel they have gotten a real workout.

Grace notes and trills as in many J.S. Bach pieces.

MIDI = Music Instrument Digital Interface (5 pin din plug)

A few tips if you are using electronics. You will likely want a controller keyboard (or master) that has excellent "action." This means it is velocity-sensitive, and feels like a real piano. It is very easy to then connect a MIDI cable to a sound unit, you can get inexpensive little keyboards with great sounds very inexpensively! Plug the MIDI into the controller's MIDI OUT, and the sound unit's MIDI IN. Some excellent controller keyboards have a USB jack to connect to the computer, and that is all that you need!

MIDI sequences can be stored in keyboards, computers and sequencers. It is neat to record sequences from keyboards and play with them – change tones or loop various parts. They take virtually no memory – unlike audio recordings. They make ring tones as well..

In the case that you are using amplifiers, or any of the standard electronic gadgets – mixers, recorders, mikes etc.. it is suggested that you by very prepared by having many adapters and **Y-JACKS** just in case. If you are on a shoestring budget, RCA-to-Quarter-Inch adapters and RCA cables are cheaper and smaller! If you want to play parts into a computer or sequencer, then have it play back while playing along, you may need extra MIDI cables and a MIDI JOINER. It's the same as a Y-Jack, 2 people can play the same sound unit. Make a practice of having plenty of adapters, including the 3-prong power to 2-prong, power strips and avoid worry!

Review of Chords

Triads = 1 - 3 - 5

There are 2 **basic** types of triads: major, and minor. They are determined by the 3rd. A Major chord like C Major Triad is C - E - G. The C minor triad is C - Eb – G. The 3 less common types are the suspended triad Csus4 = C - F – G, the diminished triad Cdim or C° = C – Eb – Gb, and the augmented triad Caug or C+ = C – E – G#.

Count the steps from the **root to the 3rd**. From C to E is 4 steps; a Major 3rd. C to Eb is only 3 steps, making the chord minor.

Common triads are M or m, Maj or min, for simple triad major chords just put the letter, like C or E or Bb; just add the minor to minor chords like Cm or C-.

From what you've just read, if someone asks what is the chord of Eb - G - C you should be able to tell them that it's C minor. G - C - Eb is also C minor. Triad chords are easy to figure out because there are only 3 notes and if they are in a different order it's just called an **inversion** of the chord.

7th chords = 1 - 3 - 5 - 7

There are 3 basic types of 7th chords: **M7, m7, 7**. CM or CM7=C Major 7th, Cm7=C minor 7th, C7=C (Dominant) 7th.

As a Jazz Pianist one system is the three types are played as: ❶ CM=**C 6/9** (E-G-A-D) or **CM7 add 9** (B-D-E-G), ❷ Cm7=**Cm9** (Eb-G-Bb-D OR Bb-D-Eb-G), ❸ C7=**C13** (E-A-Bb-D) or (Bb-D-E-A). If you can remember these 2 inversion of these 3 chord types, you can follow along most chord changes (other than diminished and altered).

Extended chords = 1 - 3 - 5 - 7 - 9 - 11 - 13

This is where it get's tricky. When you are dealing with TRIADS and 7ths you can figure out most any song's progressions or changes pretty easily, and there's some room, in case you like to do your 2-5-1's as 4-5-1's and so forth. When you venture into these chords you had better have your musical hat on and be ready to hear someone else's version on the circle of fifths, what a resolving chord is, and how songs are phrased.

Basically, you have the 2 types of triad chords above, and the 3 types of 7th chords above. In extended chords you have so many more because a C that is implying domanant could be C, C7, C9, C13, C6, C add 9, C7 add 9, C6/9, and other people might have other names for that type. There is a chord type called altered, and Calt could be C7, C7(b5), C7(+5), C7(b5b6), C7(b9), C7(+9), C7(b5b9), C7(+5b9), C7(b6b9), C7(b5b6b9), and there are still all those options for the 11th and 13th. I think the best scale to play over altered chords is fully diminished scale 1-2 starting right above the root, for example Calt being C-Db-Eb-E-Gb-G-A-Bb-C -- You'll have to practice a 9 notes per octave timing for your runs...

The best way to learn these chord types and progressions is to know, and play the circle of fifths. There are many ways, the most common being CM - Am - Dm - G7. That's 1-6-2-5 in C. The next circle or pattern to work on is Am - D7 - GM - CM - Gbm(b5) - B7(b9) - Em - E7. That is also called 2-5-1-4-7-3-6 (in the key of G). Practice these changes in all keys, all chord inversions, different tempos and you will sound great!

Percussionist Roles

Overview: Instruments' names *are* their roles

Percussion instruments and their musical roles are often the same. For example, the clave is the name of the instrument, and it's pattern. Playing correct is called being "In Clave" or if you are not, someone will say: "In Clave!" In the New World, African music understanding merged with the Europeans and created new forms that didn't exist before. The amazing thing about Latin Music is that it follows percussionist, therefore African, musical rules and approaches to composition, arrangement, and ensembles. A key component of this new mixture was that skilled percussionists have many techniques that are not found in the majority of European musics.

Claves,   Conga Drums,   Shekere,   Wood Block

Some basic ground rules would be: Parts (and the people that play them) will all be on one rhythmic focus, or clave. Other parts will focus on another rhythmic tension, repeated pattern with another accent or focus. How these two groups interact, is what the composer, arranger and quality performer set up.

A main rule that is broken is the accidentally playing the other groups pattern or emphasis, and being told "turn it over!" or "turn it around!" Friendships have been stressed, parties made less fun and other un-fun things because people don't know where their part fits in the big picture. Am I to compliment the low drum tone, or the counter-rhythm percussionist's part, or a melodic line?
It is better to know well and very clearly which side of the pattern you are supposed to be on, and who's musical toes to not step on!

Clavitos, Claves For Beginners

Clave is the key. Quite literally! That's what the word means in spanish. The instrument is made of 2 sticks, about one foot long and one inch thick. They make the very loud click that is the metronome in salsa and latin music, and much more. They can be likened to the instrument "Wood Block" which usually has just about the same rhythmic function; a loud, clear and obvious tempo mark that is heard even when it is not there!

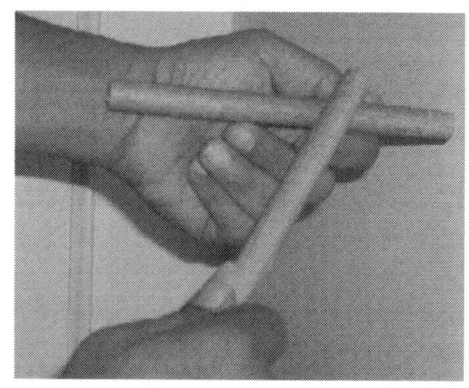

This section will include the project of having students get used drum sticks from a drummer that they like (they are always throwing away a lot of drumsticks!), then cutting them into halves, sanding them down, optionally painting them!

The Clavitos are perfect size for beginners, and they hardly have any sound at all unless you learn exactly how to palm one, then carefully tap it in the right way with the other one.

Rumba

Drumming and dance of the poorer people from the Caribbean, particularly Cuba and Puerto Rico, mostly of African descent. No melodic instruments (usually). Conga drums with 3 specific roles: Primo=basic downbeat, Segundo=basic pattern beats, and Quinto=improvised solo, a higher tone. The 3 forms of Rumba are: Guaguanco, Columbia and Yambu. Usually includes the following percussion instruments: Claves, Palito, Shekere, sometimes Agogo (or Cowbell). Each instrument has the role called by its name, for example, the palito pattern could be played on something else, like the quinto, or cowbell. Since it was developed in the Caribbean, the language is Spanish, as are the melodies.

Montuno

Latin piano part, often on guitars, violins or horns. Has 2 distinct functions: 1) Usually has a "down-side" and "up-side," not always the same down side as other instruments. 2) Defines the chord progression, usually with the leading tone as the montuno's octave note (sometimes with both hands making 4 leading tones!) or the root, 3rd or 5th. Has to be rhythmically exact, and create the perfect rhythmic tension. It is a musical / tonal instrument performing a percussionist's function.

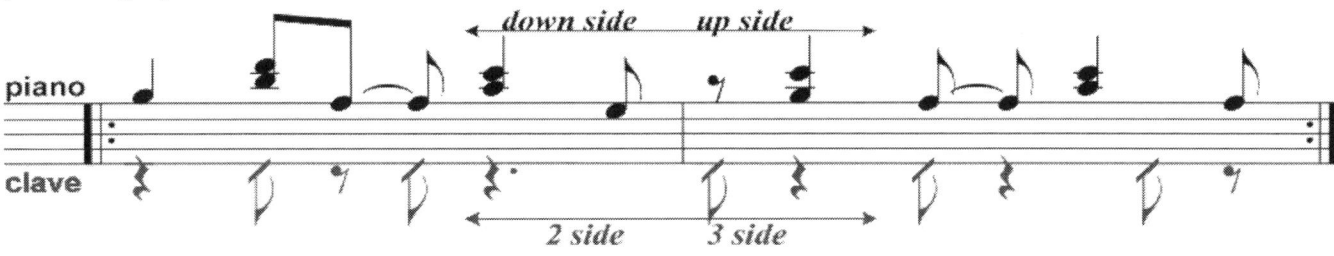

Clave Offenders

Since the most common problem is playing on the wrong side of clave, we will focus on those areas to keep you from being a clave offender. Notice from the graphic below how the Segundo conga part focuses on the beginning of bar one. It's three beats are at the beginning, it is called "in 3-2 clave." The clave part, though, focuses on the other bar, in the first bar there are only the 2 notes! It is "in 2-3 clave." The palito part, and shaker parts, should be "on the same side."

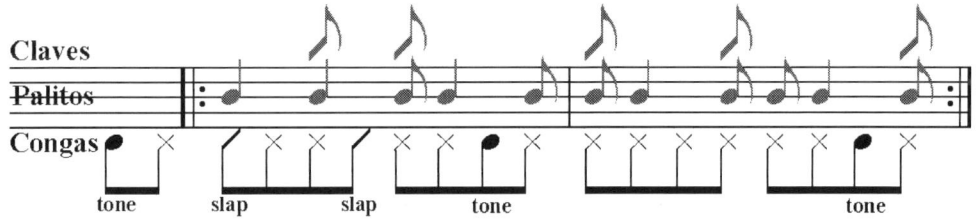

Percs 1: Da-dada-da-da

What is the answer to "Da dada da da?" Let them guess for a while, and make it fun. No, it is not Morse Code, though it looks exactly like it. The answer is "Da Da!" which is the ending of many songs, symphonies and sonatas as well. Like the last 2 notes: Ta-da!

This is "Call and Response" that is famously in African music, percussion, and so many styles of music.

Also Solo and Chorus very often (and beautifully) do trade offs, "rounds" are like this as well..

This lesson's focus is that there is a "call" side of clave, and an "answer" side. The answer side is downbeats.

Have half of the students all do the **Call** part. Have the other half do the **Answer**.

Try other phrases that are designed as clave patterns:

"Shave and a haircut, two bits."

One phrase that we've designed that is very positive is in clave pattern as well:

"Peace ease and clarity, for me."

Percs2: Clave Down!

This graphic gives you a very clear demonstration of where the clave beats are in relation to the downbeat. The claves are the clapping hands images, the downbeat is the tapping foot image.

1	2	3	**4**	**5**	6	**7**	8	**9**	10	**11**	12	**13**	14	15	16
👏			👏			👏				👏		👏			
👟				👟				👟				👟			

You can look at the clave pattern as 16 16th notes, making one bar, or 2 bars of 8th notes. A fast song usually is thought to have a "2 Bar Clave" and that is the best way for you to understand it. One bar – or side – has 3 pulses, the other bar has 3 pulses.

The above graphic is called a "3 – 2 Clave" and you can clearly see why. Sometimes you will think of the clave pattern "upside town" or "turned over" or "turned around," and that will be a "2 – 3 Clave."

First, get familiar with playing the clave and tapping the beat with your foot.

Next, be able to play the clave on a table or your leg in one hand and the pulse or beat in the other. Switch hands too!

Finally, be able to play the clave without playing the downbeat, or playing the beat in your mind only.

Listen to songs and play the clave pattern along with the song! See if you can stretch and slow down to make twice as many claves, or less longer claves. A clave can even be ½ bar, or 4 bars! Try it!

Percs3: Son Clave + Pulse

If you are not familiar with music notation, try counting the units such as: 3, 3, 4, 2, 4.

"One Bar 3-2 Clave"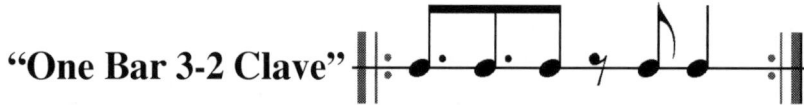

This is one way to write a one bar clave, there are others but this will do. The following is written in 2 bars, and includes the downbeat on Agogo or Cowbell.
The pulse or downbeat should be in your mind, but you can play it as well if you like.

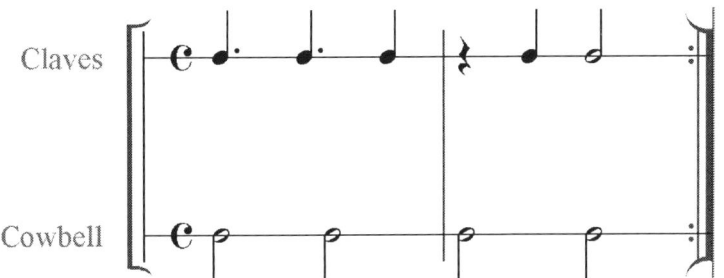

The "2 side" of the pattern is the "Down Side." It has more downbeats, and the down beat is pronounced. A "2-3" pattern has the down beat first, or the down beat side first.

Once you are playing the pattern, it will sound exactly the same, whether or not it is 2-3 or 3-2 **to you**. It **is** exactly the same to you, but in the overall arrangement it couldn't be more different.

Percs4: Palito (Simple and Basic)

Again, just like the clave pattern is named after the instrument, the palito pattern or little stick pattern mean the same thing.

This is the simple – **one bar palito**:

In fact, you can see that it is a 2 beat pattern repeated.

This is the basic **2 bar palito**:

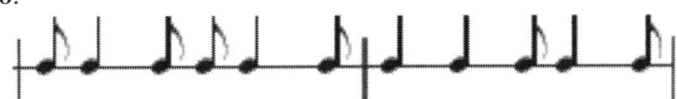

Look carefully, surely you can see which side or bar is the 2 side, meaning which is the **DOWNBEAT** side. Once you can see in that palito pattern which side is the down side, you know where the clave goes.

This palito is common in many percussionist styles, including Brazilian, Calypso, Salsa and even Boleros – ballads. It is very nice to play by simply rubbing your palms together!

Once you can play these palitos with either hand, using various fingers, it is infectious! You will find yourself tapping really nice palitos almost anytime. Keep note of which side is the down side!

You may want to end your palitos playing with the "Da da!" we learned before, think of it as the flamenco dancers last move, hand goes up gracefully. Ole!

Percs5: Clave & Palito in Binary (back and forth)

In the following example, the downbeat pattern stops for the palito part which is played with two hands.

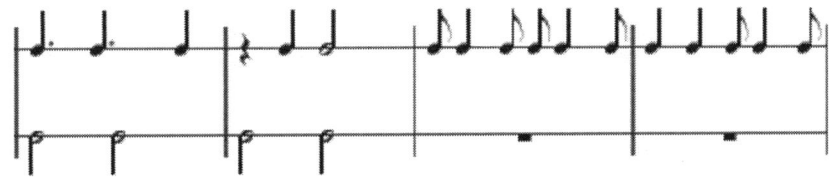

"Binary" means that you play one part for a certain amount, then the next part, back and forth.

A good idea is 4 claves, then 4 palitos, back and forth. The trick is: don't play the last little leading note of the palito pattern! It's only necessary when going back into palitos, it's not necessary for the ending, or going into the clave part again.

Percs6: Rumba Clave, Palito & Binary

Sides – claves against each other

The advanced clave is the **"Rumba Clave"** which is very similar yet very very different.

It's count is 3, 4, 3, 2, 4. The key is that the 3rd note, or "gulp," is ever so close to the 2nd half of the pattern! It is like an impossibly close note, just barely in front of the 2nd part of the pattern, and it need be accurate!

The easiest way to start learning this is to play the downbeat of the 2nd half at the same time. You can play it either with the clave pattern, or with your other hand on another instrument like a cowbell.

Eventually you can play this super-complex yet super-simple pattern without the downbeat and keep it super-tight!

Percs7: Rumba Palito

The following translation of percussion into melodic parts includes 2 opposing claves.

You will find that the Congas sounds like a 3 – 2 Son Clave pattern, in opposition to the Rumba Clave.

"Rumba Palito" a more syncopated little sticks (wood block) pattern re-envisioned into a tasty piano montuno

Percs8: Rumba Clave & Rumba Palito in Binary

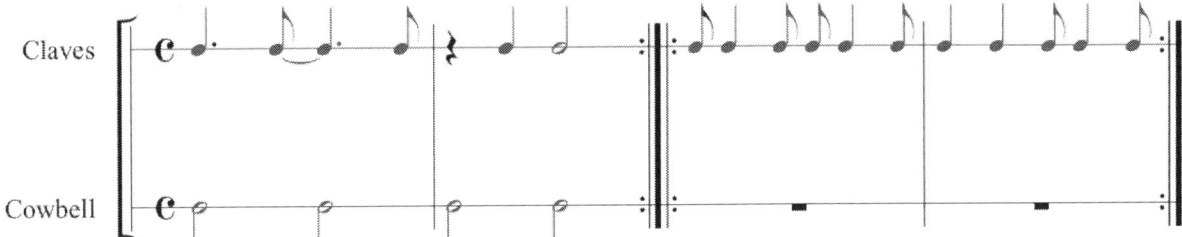

This complex Rumba Clave is similar to Son Clave but so much more exciting and fun!

"Binary" means that you play one part for a certain amount, then the next part, back and forth.

The following more advanced "Rumba Palito" should be learned after getting the basic one tight.

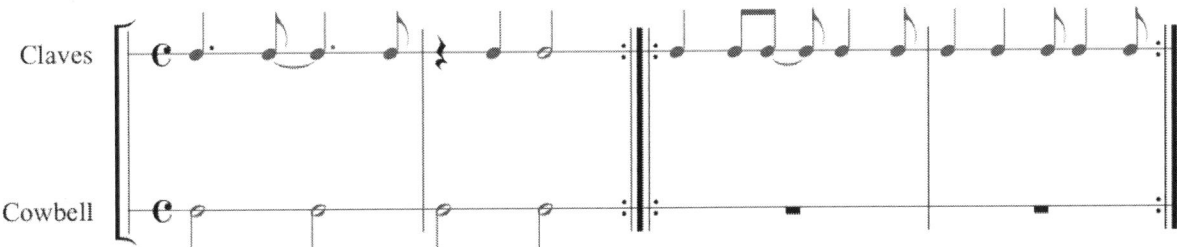

A good idea is 4 claves, then 4 palitos, back and forth.

The trick is: when going back to clave, don't play the last little leading note of the palito pattern. You may want to play it when going in to palitos.

It's only necessary when repeating palitos, it's not necessary for the ending, or going into the clave part again.

Percs9: Rumba Palito in 2-3 and Conga Dance

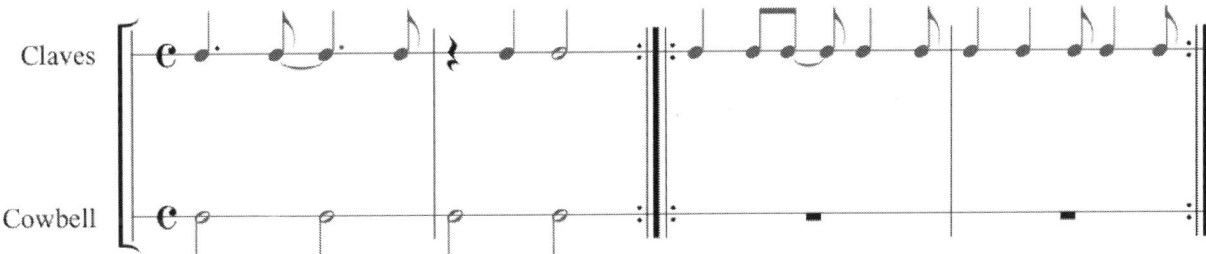

Repeat the 2nd phrase, the "Rumba Palito" by itself, but leave out the last 2 notes of the first bar.

After a while, reverse it, start on the 2nd bar.

A fun text for this is:

> "You can do the conga
>
> Everyone loves the conga
>
> You can do the conga
>
> Come and dance my conga!"

The word **conga** is the first two clave beats in the second bar. In other words the words go:

> 1 - 2 - 3 - 4 - 1 ---and!

Every other phrase can be improvised as well, allowing call and response!

Percs10: 6/8 Agogo & Cowbell Patterns

All of these patterns so far are in 4/4 time. The deeper African rhythms are in 6/8 (also called 12). There are 2 primary patterns played on **Agogo** bell, or in the new world, the **Cowbell**.

Syncopated Agogo Pattern

After understanding the 5 note clave, you will eventually see that those 5 notes are a subset, an abbreviation of much more complicated 7 note agogo patterns.

Downbeat Agogo Pattern

These are synchronized with the musical scales, the Do-Re-Mi of music in an amazing fashion. The octave is devided into 12ths, there are 12 actual notes between C and C. Of these 12 we use 7 for our scale, the 8th being the note repeated an octave away. When you play the major scale you are using whole steps and half steps. Between C and D is a whole step, but between F and G is a half step.

The Major scale is: Whole whole half whole whole whole half which if you look at the syncopated agogo pattern, is the same. The Lydian scale is: Whole whole whole half whole whole half which is the same as the downbeat agogo pattern above.

Percs20: Entries – "Counting In" With Sides

If the song is in 2 – 3 clave then the clave player – and the other instruments in sync with the clave such as the palitos, shekere and so on – will need to know how to start on the 2 side of the pattern.

Since you have been practicing both 2 – 3 and 3 – 2 patterns, it shouldn't be very difficult for you to come in either way.

Take an obvious 3 – 2 song, and count in to the song with clave and percussion

Take an obvious 2 – 3 song   probably a Rumba – count in and see the difference.

The part sounds the same, even though they are completely opposite. Funny how it is the same, and completely different at the same time hum?

Percs21: Endings – Outtros In Unison

There need be a lot of eye contact to do endings or *outtros* together, and well. The person counting will need to be ahead of everyone else, and know when to get their attention but not too soon, and definitely not too late! Then he or she should be able to let everyone know how long until the ending.

Often people will end on the clave part all together. This excerpt is from Carmen at the end of the book:

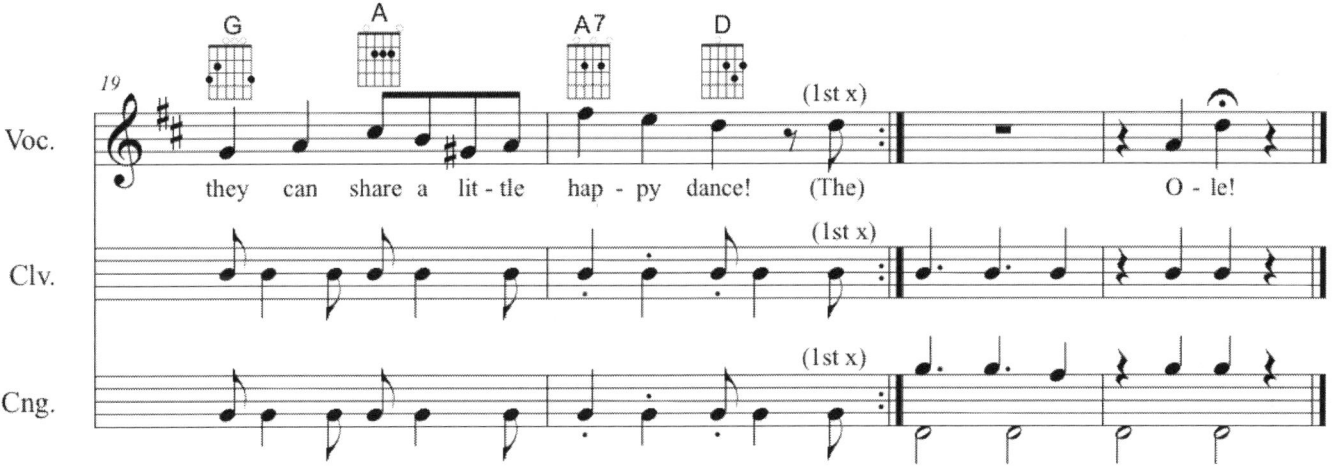

Here is a common percussion ending from Brazilian music. This is great to have the whole group do together:

Brazilian Unison Outtro

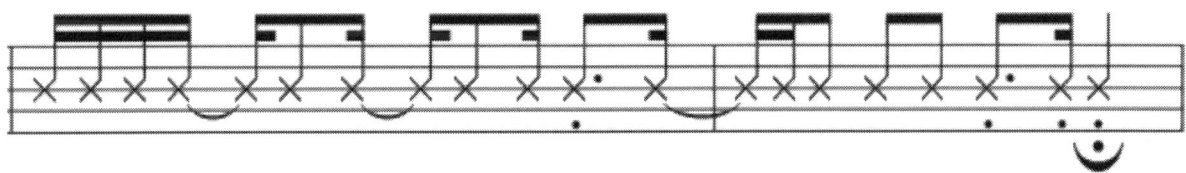

Percs22: Hearing Songs' Claves & Sides

Now when you hear a song you like, try playing various clave patterns and see which fits best! Then you can add the other perts such as palito, agogo, and perhaps even the conga drum parts.

Most songs will not have the opposing-claves technique, so don't worry about that. As far as pop or simple songs go, don't worry about being on the side of one percussion section or another, it can be considered all one unified rhythmic section.

World Music Stories

Salsa is Spanish and West African (mostly). Funny the Spanish already had an African influence from the Moors. It used the Middle Eastern Scale and interestingly, this scale *is not* West African like the rhythms of Salsa are.

Many *New World* musics are pioneers of World Music. The Trinidad people, from a great oil producing country, turned the ghastly old oil drum into, what? The amazingly beautiful Steel Drum Piano! What a gift this is!

Perhaps Wolfgang Amadeus Mozart was the first World Musician with his Turkish Rondo, but Johann Sebastian Bach had gathered suites of French and other dances and re-presented them, *the great sharing of World Music*.

Percussion Patterns Made into Melodic Phrases

In the following song the Shekere pattern is turned into the piano montuno. It is a one-bar-pattern, the simplest way to do a montuno, and there is no wrong side to it. It is more of a Cha-cha-cha montuno.

World Music Definitions of Afro-Latin Music Percussion Roles & Rules

Bembe: a religious event of the Nigerian Yoruba people. Drummers play 3 Batá drums. Batá have 2 drum heads. Each of the three drums has very specific roles. There are also usually agogo (or cowbell) patterns, shekere (or shaker) patterns, and clave patterns.

Cha-cha or Cha cha cha: slower Latin Music, also: the sound the feet make on 3-4-1 beats.

Clave: 1) wooden sticks held in a specific way to get good tone, 2) a rhythmic tension pattern, usually 5 hits. A seeming simple but quite complicated rhythmic pattern repeated endlessly. Must be accurate! One might say about your musical part: "You are not in clave!" which means that the part you are playing does not go well with clave (the montuno down side should not be on the down side of clave, see Montuno).

Diaspora: Cultural legacy. Where the peoples have traveled and influenced with their culture.

Floriano (flowery) instead of sparse parts, more notes are played, flowing.

Latin Music: from "Latin America," or Spanish-America, Cuba, Puerto Rico, the Dominican Republic, Peru, Chile, Mexico, etc.. Also called Salsa, Son or Mambo.

Mambo: 1) the style we usually call Latin Music. 2) a section of a song near the end, repeated.

Montuno: Latin piano part, often on guitars, violins or horns. Has 2 distinct functions: 1) Usually has a "down-side" and "up-side," not always the same down side as other instruments. 2) Defines the chord progression, usually with the leading tone as the montuno's octave note (sometimes with both hands making 4 leading tones!) or the root, 3rd or 5th. It has to be rhythmically exact, and create the perfect rhythmic tension. It is a musical / tonal instrument performing a percussionist's function.

Rumba: Drumming and dance form of the poorer people from the Caribbean, particularly Cuba and Puerto Rico, mostly of African descent. Usually with no melodic instruments. Conga drums with 3 specific roles: Primo=basic downbeat, Segundo=basic pattern beats, and Quinto=improvised solo, a higher tone. The 3 forms of Rumba are: Guaguanco, Columbia and Yambu. Usually includes the following percussion instruments: Claves, Palito, Shekere, sometimes Agogo (or Cowbell). <u>Each instrument has the role called by its name</u>, for example, the palito pattern could be played on something else, like the quinto, or cowbell. Since it was developed in the Caribbean, the language is Spanish, as are the melodies.

Salsa Romantica: A more slow-dancing Latin Music, flowing. Often love songs.

Son: the style we usually call Latin Music.

Yemaya (Yemonja): The Ocean Goddess. "The Mother of the Children of Fishes." One of the Orìshás, the Nigerian Yorùbá tribe's sacred deities. She is the ultimate symbol, the personification of motherhood.

Yoruba (Yorùbá): The largest tribe in Africa, from the Lagos area of Nigeria. Most American slaves came from there. The language is a tonal language with low, mid and high tones: Yo=mid, rù=low, bá=high. In some ways, the Yoruba culture is said to be most alive in pockets of ex-slaves such as Brazil, Cuba and certain regions of the U.S. These regions are called "the Yoruba Diaspora."

The following cleverly includes advanced translating of percussion parts into melodic phrases in pages 2 and 3.

Yorùbá Diasporas

© 1993
Teo Vincent 4th

Allegro con brio - with brilliance

syncopated yet smooth

(1) It is a harmonic delight when some or all melodic parts imply Am7-D7 while the Bass plays FM7-Dm7

Yorùbá Diasporas (page 2)

"Rumba"
"Palito" (the word means little sticks) wood block patterns turned into piano "montuno" phrase

relaxed and steady

"Segundo" drum part. The foundation of Rumba is the "Tres Golpes" of the segundo opposite the "3 side" of the rumba clave pattern

Too hot and spicy?
Skip to next pepper

Afro-Caribbean Rumba is: 3 conga drums, claves, palitos (or wood block) and singing. Usually no tonal instruments. This section is a creative adaption of the percussionist roles and rules into melodic music parts and phrases.

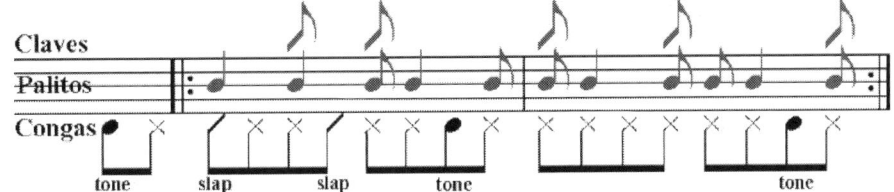

Yorùbá Diasporas (page 3)

"Rumba Clave" especially complex syncopation pattern played expressively on chromatic dissonant chords

"Rumba Palito" a more syncopated little sticks (wood block) pattern re-envisioned into a tasty piano montuno

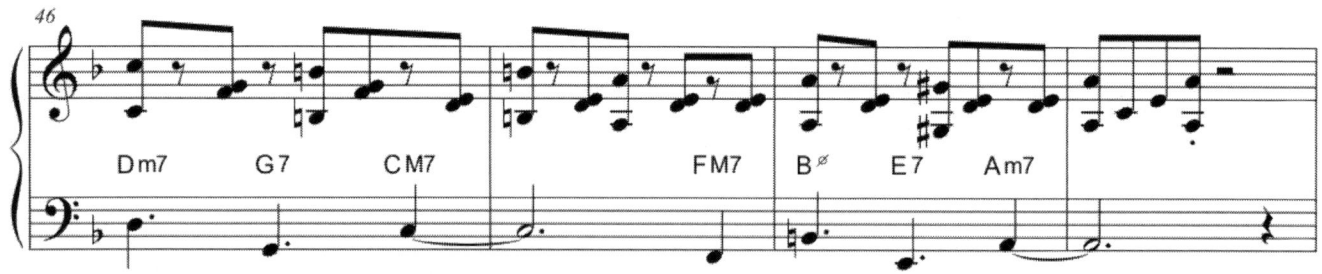

Yorùbá Diasporas (page 4)

Chromatic Montuno #1

Chromatic Montuno #2

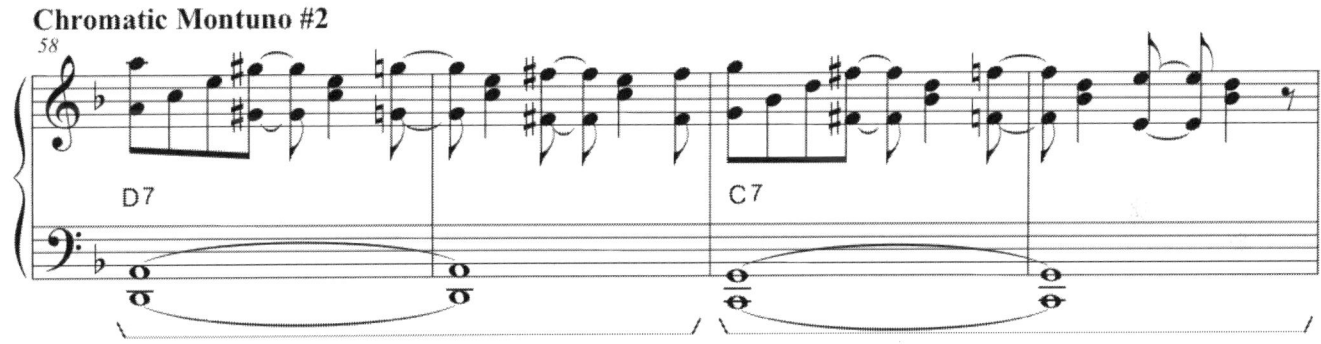

Yorùbá Diasporas (page 5)

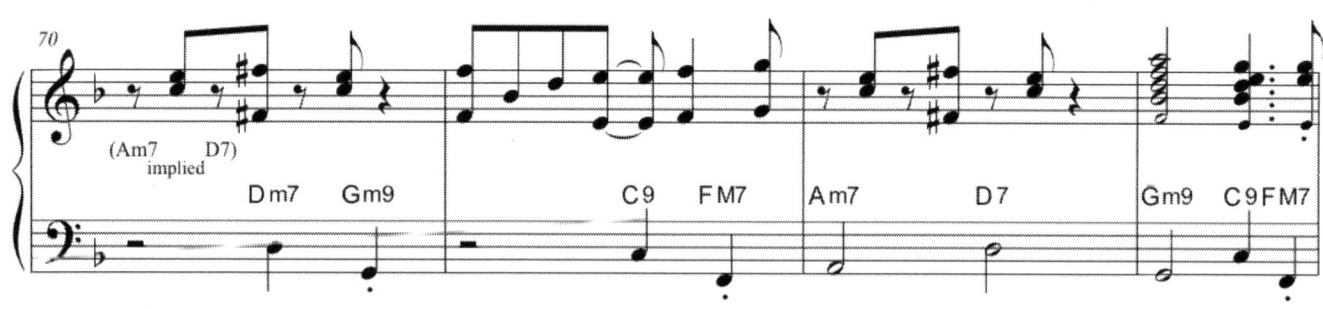

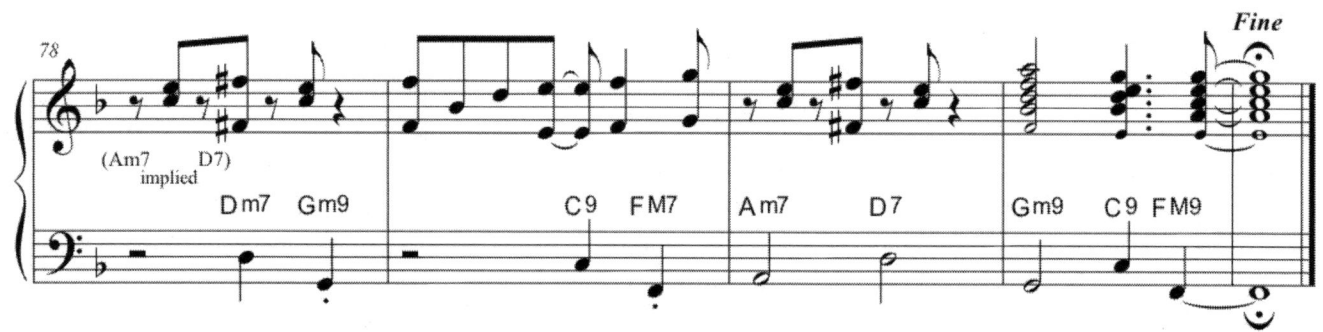

Complimenting Ensembles

One of the most advanced business techniques is to groom your successor. Rather than just keep your competition down, you help the person that will replace you, so that you move up the ladder.

The pianist's role is often to accompany the singer. By extension, the keyboardist is often giving everybody in the ensemble their part, harmonic structure, tempo and even feel or mood. In the old operas the harpsichord might be so quiet that it is drowned out by the louder instruments, but it's role is key to keeping the orchestra "in the groove."

In Jazz, the term is: The Piano *Comps*. Comping in another way of looking at it is playing the accompaniment. Comp chords are giving the harmonic structure to the basic melody and parts.

There are many reasons why an artist compliments his friends a lot: for one, if one is judged by the company that they keep, then showing their company in the best view is best for them as well! It is also just simply good to encourage the best in people, help them see their accomplishments and good points rather than focus on their weaknesses. I remember being absolutely wowed by Pat Metheny's keyboardist Lyle Wagner, but he was more the backbone, in the shadows, allowing the star to shine ever so brightly. Lyle is great at complimenting, in the best sense of the word, and the best sense of the work.

When all the parts of the ensemble are clear on the overall structure and process throughout a song, having the conductor inside each musician keeping each in their proper role and compliment to the whole, this is when everything flows gracefully and beautifully.

Highlife has: 1-Rhythm, 2-Line and 3-Lead Guitar Parts

Highlife is a beautiful and fun the West African style of dance music.

Highlife style was made popular by King Sunny Ade the great guitarist among others.

One guitar plays chords. Another plays "the line," an important part of the arrangement rhythmically *and* harmonically. The third guitar is the lead guitarist, and the lead part may be a 8 bar phrase or even longer!

Afrobeat was an important synthesis of the two: Nigerian and American Soul musics by the famous Nigerian artist **Fela Kuti**. Fela was very inspired by the American James Brown's Soul Music and guitar grooves so Afrobeat was a way of merging old and new styles.

The great Camaroonian composer Hugh Masakela did similarly with "Soul Makosa," a song popular in the 1970s. Makosa is a traditional African musical form.

Many African musicians came to California originally on tour with Hugh Masakela's band in the 1970s.

Some musicians came to California from playing with Fela. His son still leads his band.

There is a Cameroonian band that plays awesome salsa, and sings in Spanish, and doesn't even know what they are saying! Their tempos are amazingly tight though! What goes around, comes around!

The one bar pattern has no down side and up side. The following two bar patterns do have up and down sides:

Two Bar Soca (Soul-Calypso) Percussions

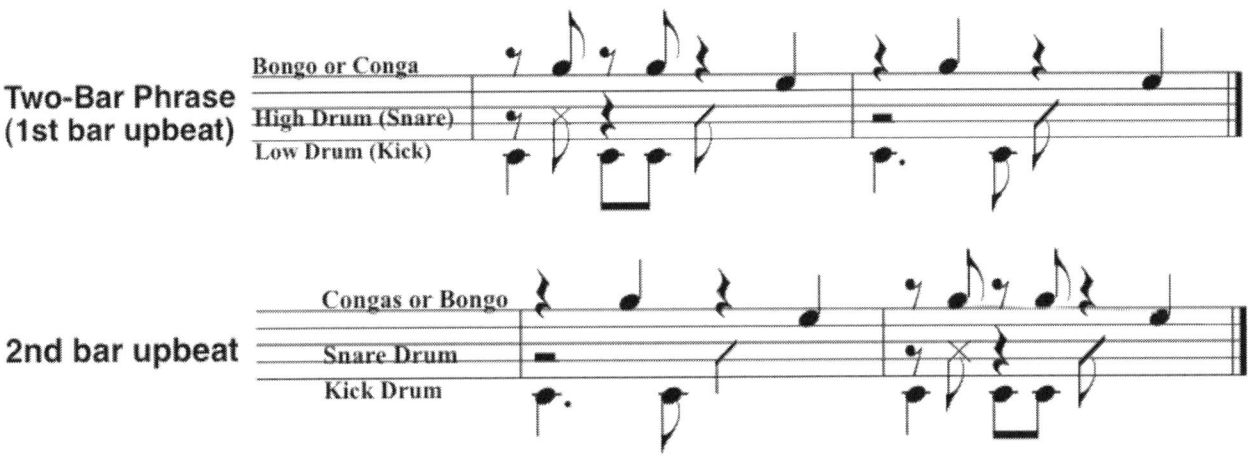

Have one person play both the low and high drum parts, repeated, and then another person come in with the bongo drum part. These things can also be sung instead of played on drums.

The kick and snare could sound like: "Boo – pootat, Bootaboopootat." The next part could be sounded like "bing, bong, bingbing, bong."

Then reverse the patterns: The kick and snare are: "Bootaboopootat, Boo – pootat" and the bongo is: "bingbing, bong, bing, bong."

After trying the above examples, you can see clearly that one side is up and another is down. This helps immensely as you coordinate the group to play and sound good together.

Can you see that just like a clave pattern, both of the two bar patterns are identical except for where they start?

Rhythm Section Accompaniment "Chucks"

Notice how the piano part and guitar chords have accent on the first beat – by following it immediately, not at all like the 2nd half extremely on-the-beat. We can assume therefore, that their "down" side is the 2nd half, in other words, the accompaniment to Calypso Study #1 is in "3-2 clave."

Also notice that the melody highlights the clave pattern on the second side, as Jazz chords often do. Unlike the accompaniment, the melody is clearly in a phrase that is in "2-3 clave." This combination means that the musicians don't step on each other's foot, they leave the all important spaces!

The guitar to be right after the 1 is a special Soca (Soul-Calypso) technique that makes the rhythm very bouncy, well, how else could Trinidadians, "Trinys," win so many carnival competitions? To dance for hours with heavy costumes and such, special bouncy Soca "Guitsy Riddim" keeps you up (and up beat)!!

Yemaya Orisha Ocean Goddess

Moderato, tempo giusto - exact timing

© 2006
Teo Vincent 4th

World Music Compilation 48

Yemaya Orisha Ocean Goddess (2)

Yemaya Orisha Ocean Goddess (3)

The *Yoruba* People from Nigeria, West Africa

To be totally correct it is actually Yorùbá: The largest tribe in Africa, from the Lagos area of Nigeria. The Yoruba are the most traveled around the world historically. The majority of American slaves came from there. The language Yorùbá is a tonal language, low mid and high tones: Yo=mid, rù=low, bá=high.

In some ways, the Yoruba culture is said to be most alive in pockets of ex-slaves such as Brazil, Cuba and certain regions of the U.S. These are called "the Yoruba Diaspora."

Some *Afro-Latin Music* definitions:

Latin America basically means Spanish America: Cuba, Puerto Rico, the Dominican Republic, Panama, Argentina, Columbian, Nicaragua, El Salvador, Peru, Chile, Guatemala, Mexico, etc.. mostly Catholic cultures.

Latin Music is from Latin America. It is also called Salsa, Cha-cha, Son or Mambo. Although it is a long distance, both physically and culturally, the rhythm in Latin Music is or has African roots. Latinos all know this, and they are quite proud of the African drums and culture mixed into their music.

Sadly, people in the United States often don't know how rich Latin music is with deeply loved African roots. This is partly because under slavery in the US drums were illegal, as was speaking any African language or doing things resembling African culture – though in some rare cases some survived.

A ***Bembe*** is a religious event of the Nigerian Yoruba people. Drummers play 3 Batá drums. Batá are sacred drums that have 2 drum heads. Each of the three drums has very specific roles. Other percussion instruments are often agogo (or cowbell) patterns, shekere (or shaker) patterns, and clave patterns.

Songs are to honor their deities called "**Orishas**." Sometimes they (and the religion itself) are called "The Seven Powers," though there are many orishas and they have wonderfully interesting stories and interactions with each other! Chango is the warrior and lover. Yemaya the ocean goddess. Osain the owner of herbs. Ochossi is the hunter. Ogun rules metals. Elegbara (or Elegua or Eshu) is the trickster. Oya the wild woman of the cemeteries. Ochun the Love Goddess. Others are: Orunmila the owner of the divination system or "Table of Ifa," Obatala the ruler of the head, Orunmila Goddess of the Heavens, Ibeji The Twins.

They have been "syncretized" with the Catholic Saints. Chango is Santa Barbara (both have the colors red and white), Niño de Atocha is Eshu, Virgin de Caridad del Cobre is Oshun, etc.. This way the followers could pray to Chango but tell master that they were praying to Santa Barbara.

This Nigerian language and culture in the new world is called "**Lukumi**" which is a word in the Yoruba language which means "friend." This is simply to distinguish it from it's Nigerian roots. This culture is quite alive and vibrant in many parts of the new world. See the movie "**Quilombo**" about Brazilian escaped slaves to see good examples of the Yoruba Orishas / Dieties.

The integration of the roots of salsa – Nigerian Yoruba tribe's music – into modern, new world music, is a thrilling blend of old and new, earthy and sophisticated, tribal and social, that is immensely entertaining and also greatly educational and uplifting for many people who have lost the connection with their roots.

The Yemaya song just above is adapted for singing and percussion at the end of the book. As a piano solo it is allowed more flexible time: bars 17 & 18 disappear – the agogo pattern shifts sides, but doesn't on the same part of page 3. The idea was crashing ocean waves in the first section, calm water softly flowing (even bar sets) at the end.

"Afro-Blue" the Jazz song is an Orisha song to Obatala (king of the head) that has been adapted & converted to African-American popular, non-religious, ***secular music.***

Motifs and Motivations

Pianist Anton Kwerti talking about Beethoven's 5th piano concerto: "Beethoven used the Salami style of composing. He chops the motif into little pieces like a salami, and you want to pick up the pieces off of the floor."

The "word" in music is the motif. Put them together and you get sentences, paragraphs etc.. You may read it as *motif* in one book, *motive* in another, they are the same thing! In LVB's 5th Symphony we have the classic motif of S-S-S-L-- (short short short long), perhaps the most well known motif of all (It was written just as he was losing his hearing and some think it is "I can not **hear!**" or "Why make me **deaf?!**"). If we expand the motif to s-s-s-l-s-l-s-l then we get a phrase that begs an answer. It motivates you to reply.

Beethoven't 5th becomes a Perpetual Motivator

Call and Response / Rhythmic Balance in Latin Music

The "**Tumbau,**" the rhythm that dancers so love in Latin Music of Bass & Montuno is Rhythmic Counterbalance. The accented quarter note in the left hand with the eighth note accent in the right hand is extremely complex and difficult even for virtuoso classical pianists (bar 5 of "Montuno Etude" in a few pages).

An excellent exercise for the whole group is the beautiful fun song: *Sandungera* by the group *Los Van Van*.

Calypso and Zouk styles of music often have the bass guitar accent the 3 and 4 of the phrase. If you listen to West African Highlife, you will often hear this same accent.

What African and African rooted music gives you is the rhythmic tension that makes you want to hear the completion of the pattern, the answer, musically, rhythmically.

In addition to the magic of beats of rhythm propelling you up to dance and sing, the beauty and grace of masterful music played by energetic and vibrant performers motivates you to share your own beauty and grace with the world. Get inspired and get involved in motivating music!

Afro-American Contributions

"Latin Music" is Black Man's heritage. Latinos know that it is African rhythms in their music. Even so African that it throws you off, you are lost unless you really know it, like traditional complex African music.
In the U.S. drums was illegal. They thought the slaves could communicate and plan revolts. African music and culture was thoroughly removed! What is suppressed, repressed and held back re-emerges. "*What you resist persists!*" Inevitably the African sense of rhythm and it's divinity naturally arose in Afro-American culture.

Louisiana was French - blacks could play drums in "Congo Square" on Sundays. This is one reason why so much of Afro-American music is from New Orleans, Louisiana.

    1st Contribution-> Singing & soul wrenching excitement, even possession by (the holy) spirit inserted into the black Baptist church.

    2nd Contribution-> Drum balance re-emerging generations later. The Rhythmic Tension of drum parts re-invented and evolved. Drums made into harmonic, melodic musical parts and phrases. Sections arranged as if they were percussion sections or following percussionist rules.

Play the rhythm 3-3-2 with the chords: C-E-G. In the other hand play in the spaces, that is a **One Bar Pattern**.

Syncometric Foundations = 1st and 2nd drums (primero y segundo), that's **Two Bar Patterns** like the bass below.

All About The Bass

The Herbie Hancock song Chameleon demonstrates 2 bar patterns perfectly. The bass part = drum patterns – in this case the claves, as shown below. The solo = contrary rhythmic feel, contrast.

The solo in Caribbean drums is: **Quinto** = embellishments like in Jazz. Spanish words are often used because Latin Americans know this. They know their music has African rhythms.

Brazilian Rimshot-Clave is a great foundation under solos. Play chords in the circle of fifths with the rhythm and the solos are easy to come up with, and interrelate beautifully.

From Disco to R&B, Salsa to Merengue, it is the African counter-rhythms that make the layers of "Latin Music" that is so popular. It is playing on instruments the 1st drum parts, 2nd drum, (primero and segundo) and other percussion parts becoming the embellishments beautifully interwoven.

Perpetual Motivations

A core component of the joy of making music together is having a repertoire of parts that can be played by one musician over and over, that give rhythmic and harmonic foundation so clearly defined that it is almost effortless for other musicians to hear opportune places to add phrases. These are germs – basics that germinate into full blown group motifs or collective motivations. The shortcut for these is: "Motorvations."

Cuba used to have a great musical influence over not only the United States but really the whole world. Their big bands and extravagant nightclubs are famous and well known. Much of their music allowed the African musical sensibilities to bring percussion parts into melodic music, creating repeated patterns that really add a fresh earthiness to music.

In the United States African ancestry people who were not allowed to keep their African instruments, language or culture, still brought rhythmic patterns and repeated longer motifs to the music that is now simply American music such as Jazz.

If you listen to good bass patterns in Afro-American music they act as motifs to build upon, very much like classical orchestrations in symphonies, fugues and concertos.

Many African Americans will tell you that the music moves them to a place where they feel more at home. It moves them inside and in their hearts. There are amazing intrinsic ways that the African relationship with music has secretly been released in American music!

The following two scales almost magically synchronize African agogo patterns with the most common major scales. The 2 most common agogo patterns, and the 2 most common major scales!

Syncro-Nice Sacred Rhythm Scales

Major scale above, Lydian below

Conversation Pieces Solo: 1) Chords arpeggiated 2) Scales 3) Chromatic

Very Slow

In general you can use the song "Heart And Soul" as a performance project because it is a recognizable well known foundation for repeatable parts that include Call and Response. It is also potent for solos – improvisation creation.

The Montuno is a Great Motorvator

The Latin Music Motorvation is the "Montuno." The Montuno defines firstly the rhythmic phrase in terms of which side it plays and it's floweriness or floriano quality (sparseness or fullness). Secondly the montuno defines the chord progression pretty fully. A complete and concise montuno will lean prominently on the leading tone from chord to chord making harmonic progression confusion impossible.

If you play a good montuno, especially with the "Tumbao" or bass pattern that is derived from African drum patterns, often it will motivate someone to start playing percussion, or even joining in with a song that they know that fits over the pattern you are playing.

If you know 5 or 10 various montuno patterns, you can be the center of a musical experience where everyone wants to join in and sing, dance, improvise, and compose complimentary parts and phrases creating collaborative new music in real time!

This type of real-time composing and improvising is one of the greatest ways that humans can act collectively to play their part and improve the whole. Again, the seeds of this type of group performance is repeated motifs of a specific design, which we are bringing to you in useful functions as Perpetual Motivators.

Montuno Etude No. 1

Dedicated to Oszkar Morzsa

2011
Teo Vincent IV

World Music Compilation 55

Swing Montuno Study

Allegro capriccioso - lively & playful

Teo Vincent 4th

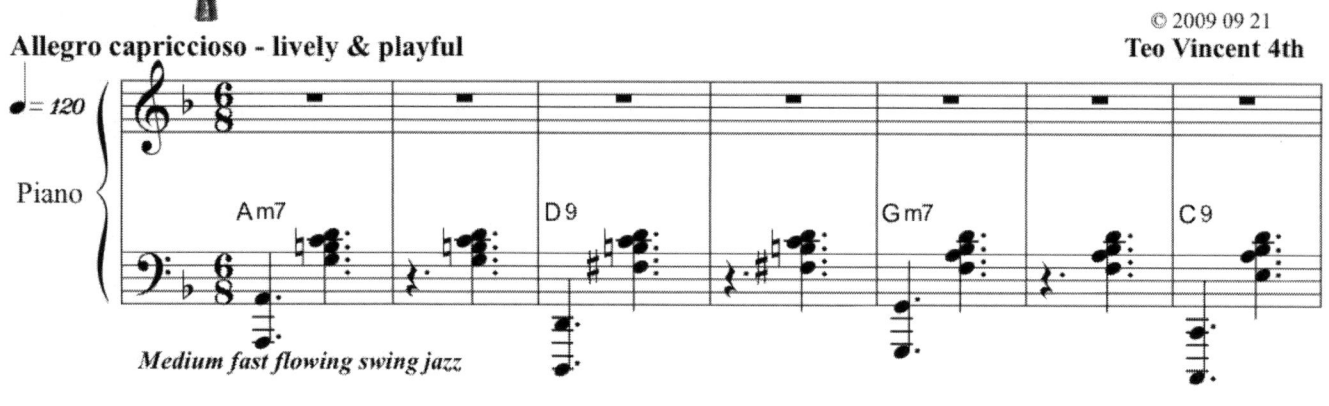

Medium fast flowing swing jazz

Swing Montuno Study (2)

- A montuno's role is to define the rhythmic form AND the harmonic form. The play with the rhythmic tension in 4/4 is quite complex enough for most. In swing, 6/8, it is a Herculean challenge, but musically thrilling.

- The African 6/8 "Bembe Agogo" (Cowbell) pattern has the pulse (downbeat) plus Clave, use this first.

- Great percussionists imply and substitute 6/8 patterns into songs in 4/4. Try doing it with these montunos.

Bembe Percussion Roles

That Makes This Heaven

Teo Vincent IV
(c) 2011

World Music Compilation 58

TIGHT SCHOOL

Here we tie a few things together smoothly by sharing with you techniques to give you enhanced overview of songs inner rhythmic phrases and arrangements. This information will help serious music artists to be able to 'get inside' the music, and have clean tight chops that don't step on anyone else's part. These rules may not apply to your style or musical level but are useful rules to know. You may not play "Latin Music," but the montuno studies below can be applied to any form of music and will help you be a complementary musician and a complementing sound.

In this lesson we are reviewing and building on the rules for playing the MONTUNO - Salsa Piano part correctly depending on how the CLAVE pattern is played (the pattern for the little sticks that hold the meter, feel and pulse in Cuban music). The CHUCKS area below this one describes other ways to be on the correct side of the musical phrase as well.

Review: The Correct Side Of The Pattern

The clave pattern has definite sides. It is the most efficient way to learn the sides of musical patterns by learning clave rules. When you are talking about the sides of the pattern you are talking **percussionist rules**, or standards. For example, a part of the kinto solo in guaguanco Afro-Cuban Drumming requires that the kinto solo does not step on the clave part at all, no note of the solo can be the same as the clave's. This is a concentrated syncopation technology where the soloist not only embeleshes the pattern but... tries to confuse it. I've seen cat's pull the timing two ways from sunday while a master percussionist is just trying to hold the clave pattern and it is not an easy rhythm to hold!

Tres Golps (3 gulps or 3 pulses)

That's the first half of a clave pattern. Here you will see it in one bar and two bar charting. Jazz and Salsa is usually in CUT TIME, so the count is twice as fast. These graphics are in both types, because the percussion rules are the same.

Remember there are considered to be 2 general clave patterns, son clave and rumba clave ("Bembe Clave" is so complex, get to that later). Both of these clave's can be played in **3 - 2 or 2 - 3**, this is called the clave being on one side or the other.

2-3 RUMBA CLAVE

The 3 side of the clave is the down side. A 3-2 clave pattern has the down side at the beginning of the phrase instead of in the middle. The rule, and you will find it a tough one, is to never play your montuno or rhythm part on the down side of clave. The following pattern, your basic C 1 - 4 - 5 - 4 montuno,

should not be played against a 3-2 clave, instead you would use one like this:

You can see that the second montuno is up on the down side of clave. You could also use a montuno where both sides are UP, and that montuno fits over any clave!

That gives you powerful concepts to think about, and years of things to practice.

CHUCKS (Accompaniment Accenting One or the Other Side)

Background and underlying rhythms are often called chucks. A good way to understand how they compliment the basic rhythmic pulse is to theck out how they can be on one side of the rhythm or the other.

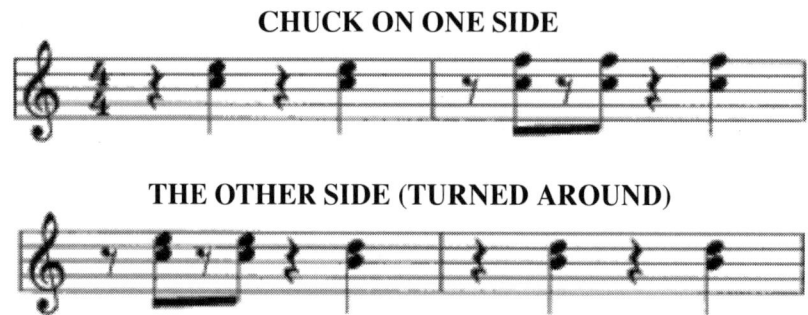

Play even just a C Major chord with these rhythms, you will see the difference in feel, and different ones (different sides) can be used in different parts of arrangements.

DESIGNING MONTUNOS

In these lessons bass parts are written in treble clef for simplicity; once you learn them take them down at least one octave. The 3 montunos above would be played over a tumbau or bass pattern like this:

So put the tumbau in your left hand, then add the montuno in the right.
The following shows more bass and piano parts fundamental to montuno theory:

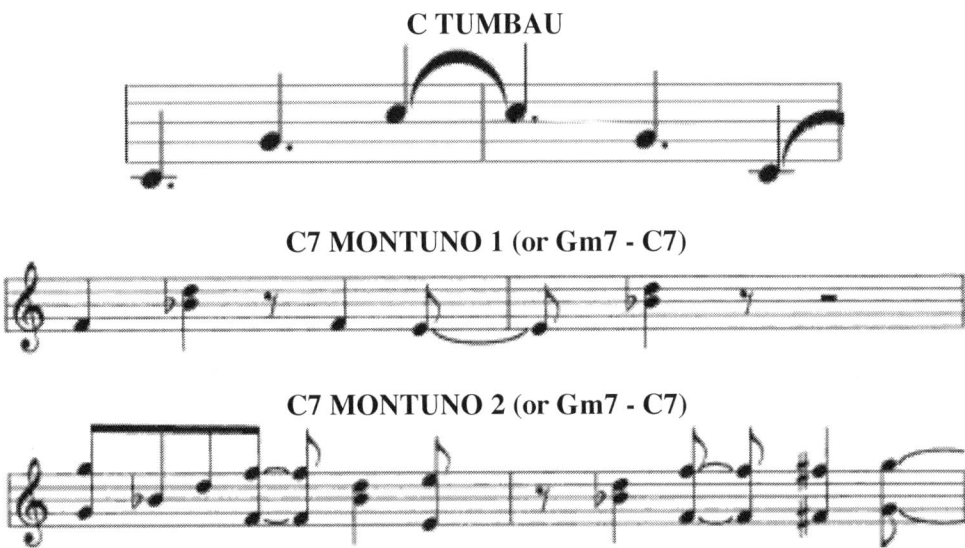

In montuno design you will find that the montuno plays a primary role in the rhythmic role of a song or progression and also a primary melodic role. When singers are getting their parts together it is often necessary for them to hear the chords, and chord progressions; often a piano or guitar is the only instrument necessary for this. Montunos do all of that - show the harmonic pattern as well as the rhythmic pattern. As explained above, the montuno should be correctly layered on top of the rhythmic pulse.

To also compliment the basic melodic aspects of the song the montuno is based on the leading tones of the chords. So if the chords go from Gm to C7 the leading tones are Bb and F to Bb and E (the 3rd and 7th of both chords). You will see that that is almost exactly what C montuno 1 does above. The following example shows this even better, the leading tones in C 1 - 6 - 2 - 5 are B&E, A&E, C&F, B&F. Notice how that is exactly what the following montuno does, you could even take out the G and A on top of the piano part and it still is perfect as a montuno, defining the rhythmic arrangement and the melodic arrangement.

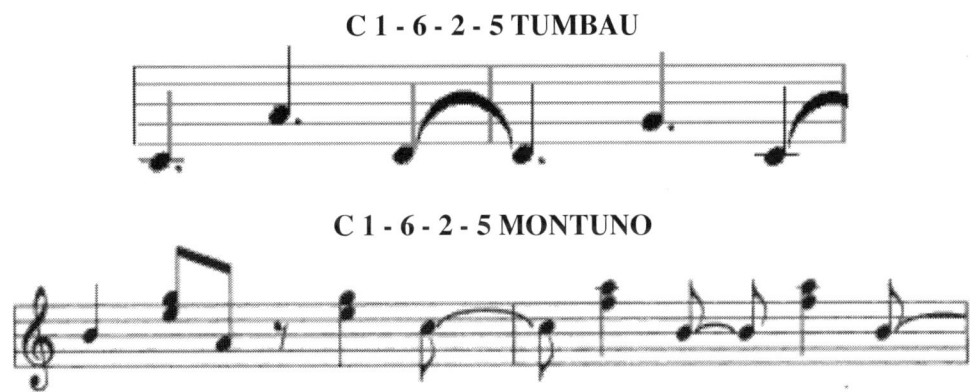

The above is a great practice for 1) circles of fifths, 2) left / right hand coordination, and 3) tumbau and montuno development. Once you can feel the delay in the montuno, against the bass hand's standard 3-3-2 timing you will be feeling and learning one of the best syncopation techniques, one syncopation leading another syncopation by just a hair! Try the above in as many keys as you can.

Calypso Guitar Chucks

In Calypso and Reggae the Motorvator is the Chuck pattern of the guitar or keyboard. It's function is the same as the montuno, defining the chordal progression and the rhythmic pattern.

One distinction between Calypso and Latin music is that in Latin percussion there is more often than not a balance of components on "one side," such as 3-2, and other components that are playing "2-3," or "opposing clave," which gives the percussionists greater and greater possibilities of interacting with various instrumental sections.

Another way to say this is that in Calypso and Reggae basically all parts will have the same chuck pattern (side).

Sections, Unions & Oppositions

Calypso Circles

2010 09 24

Teo Vincent IV

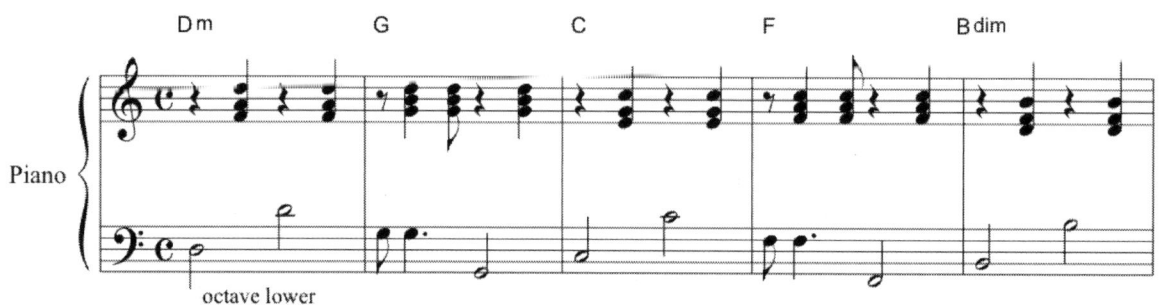

Louisiana style Second-Line chants calls and answers

The second line in the parade has a great tradition of call-and-response from the south, southern US culture.

Give half of the group one part such as: "Shoo fly, don't bother me!"

The other half the let them answer: "Go away fly and let me be."

The first part goes again, then other answers such as: "I'm going to swat you wait and see!" It can be fun!

Another one is: "Hold 'em Joe!" answered: "No don't let 'em go." "Hold 'em Joe!" "Hold mo' and mo'!"

What we have here is the basic Call and Response common to African and other World Musics. It is also Chorus and Solo or Lead, and is really almost all that there is in Orisha songs, the sacred songs of the Nigerian Yoruba people.

The great Italian Baroque composer Antonio Vivaldi (1678-1741) used a similar concept of a group and soloist having a dialog. In *concerto grosso* there are the two: "the call," *solo* and "the answer," *tutti* (or *ripieno*) which means full in Italian.

You can hear this marvelously in his "Le Quattro Stagioni" or "The Four Seasons" where you hear wonderful dialog between the lead (solo) violinist and the orchestra (Tutti / Ripieno).

Phrases

What's the *Catch-Phrase*

In technology you need to know the buzz-words. To a fine pianist, phrasing means that the melody is to be sung, sweetly. This use of phrases is where we look at groups of instruments acting together to make pleasing and charming conversations with other groups of instruments. *"Hello, how are you today?" "Just fine! Try this trick on for size?" "That is dandy, may I join?"* And on and on.

In American music we look to the rhythm section to know if we are in 2-3 or 3-2 rhythmic phrasing. Only in advanced Jazz arrangements would we have some instruments with their clave on one side and some instruments with their clave on the other.

One of the best ways to understand the arrangement of American songs is to find out where the Clavinet part would be. This is similar to finding out where the Clave pattern would be, but it includes the rhythmic progression *and* the harmonic progression. To determine the clavinet part one need be half percussionist and half accompanist. In other musics this could be similar to the accordion part, mandolin part or cavaquino (little Brazilian guitar) part.

High Life Phrasing

That is a one or two bar rhythmic phrase arranging. In African music it goes to another level of arranging rhythmic parts translated into harmonic parts. **Nigerian Highlife** has:

1) Rhythm,
2) Line and
3) Lead Guitar (Tenor Guitar)

Parts each with their specific role.

Chord or Rhythm (Riddim in Reggae Lengua) plays chords and basic percussion phrases. The Line is a part roughly equivalent to the bassline in American songs. Repeated one or 2 bar part that fits over the Rhythm part. The Lead Guitar (often called the Tenor Guitar) plays long parts often 4 bars long, or longer, similar to the song's verse.

The Nigerian artist **King Sunny Ade** has these wonderful guitar arrangements if you can listen to his group.

Hohner D-6 Clavinet

"Soca Clav" is a good example of Soca (Soul Calypso) chuck pattern, more flowery than the rhythm guitar or piano might play, but clearly defining the harmonic and rhythmic phrase

Soca Clav

Teo Vincent IV
(c) 2009 07 18 Givnology

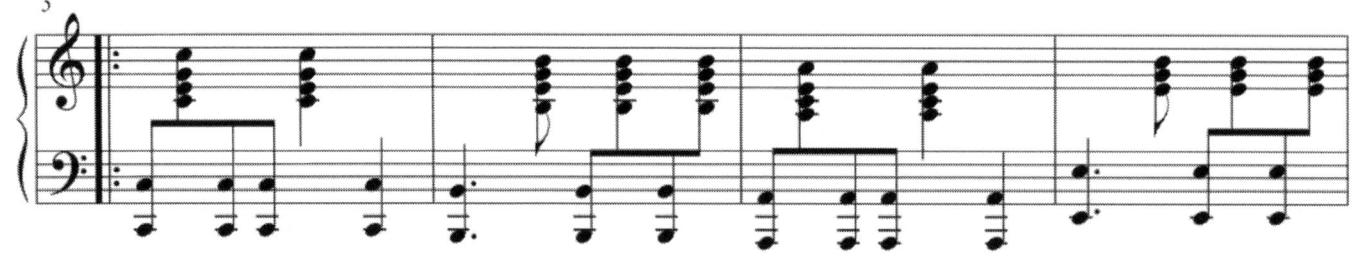

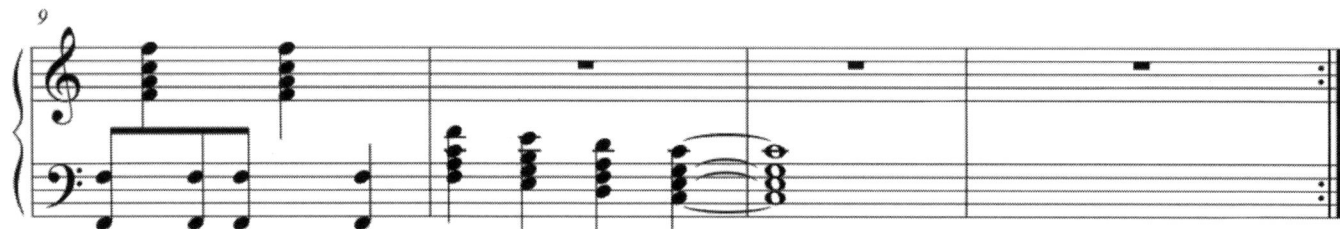

A Calypsonian friend would sing "No Woman No Cry" with the 2nd section of Soca Clav above☺.

The "SuperClav" score below demonstrates a "2-3" pattern, meaning that the first half of the phrase goes "1-**2-3**" and the second half is the "tres gulpes" or "three gulpes" of the clave pattern. In bar 13 you hear the chords played imitating the clave like the rim-shot trap drum part in Bossanova though it is "turned around." Bossa-rimshot-clave is a central focus of much of the 1970s dance music of the United States. Try this rhythm with chords to solo with!

The bass notes give us our harmonic analysis information to determine a "I I IV V" chord progression.

Super Clavinet Technique

Givnology Labs

When you can use Motorvations:

In any type of popular music ensemble, a key to sounding good is a unified beat or pulse. How to have everyone truly feel the tempo together is a great skill for having your band sound good. You can give the motorvator to a guitarist, and have other instruments come in one at a time, finding a complimentary phrase. This "buildup" is common in soul music of good instrumentalists such as James Brown, Herbie Hancock, Kool And The Gang, Stevie Wonder, The Staple Singers, etc..

The concept of Perpetual Motivations was brought together after realizing that 1) the great Italian composer Nicolo Paganini had **Perpetual Motion** studies, and the great pianist Anton Kwerti explained a "**Motif Composing Technique**" used by Beethoven, the salami method he called it, cutting the motif into little pieces then picking them up off of the floor, figuratively. Being well grounded in Afro-Caribbean percussion concepts, montunos calypso chucks and funky soul music clavinet phrases, it all adds up to just about the same thing, with the cultural variations that are natural to any artistic analysis.

Motives, motifs and motivational inspiring

The final inspiration is the epiphany or revelation that a motif is the same as a motive as in a motivational starting point. As in looking at things for what can bring them together, cohese disparate phrases into congealable wholes. We call this: **Unidiversity**, uniting in our diversity.

The correct expression of unity allows all to find a place and way to be a part, without lessening the original idea by overdoing one's originality. A perpetual motivation is the musical equivalent to a negotiator who leaves us all with lingering positive truths stuck in our ear that remind us of the great purpose of uniting our individualities into a greater whole – greater than the sum of our parts!

Giving credit

We are grateful to artists who keep cultures alive even though they are not written down. A guitarist in Nigeria might live with his teacher and do duties for his teacher like a religious follower or devotee.

Some say that "World Music" is music that has not been written down. Some Folk Music has the same distinction. What is your opinion on the topic? Does it change just because it is written down? It certainly allows more people to play it and enjoy it. Here is a true story that illustrates this idea of writing down folk music and who should get the credit:

In many cities the most often performed Opera is "**Carmen**" by Georges Bizet (1838-1875). There is the famous aria (song) that Carmen sings to seduce Don José the soldier called "**Carmen's Habanera.**" It is a masterful song, though there is an amazing history to Bizet's writing of this Habanera. We have redone it at the end of this book, adapted to teach percussion patterns with the very memorable and beautiful melody. You can also play Georges Bizet's Symphony reduction (included later in this book) to enjoy his "Eastern" composing style.

Yradier's-Bizet's-Carmen's Habanera

Can you guess where a Habanera is from? Here is one hint. In Spanish the "v" is often pronounced "b." Still can't guess? The little island of Cuba's capital city of course! Though French composer Bizet actually never went to Spain, the story goes that he composed music on a piano at the studio of Elisabeth Celeste Vernard-Chabrillan "La Mogador" (1824-1909), a writer, singer & student of Charles Gounod (1818-1893). Bizet heard her singing "El Arreglito" by Sebastien Yradier (1809-1865) *born Iradier*. (Celeste Mogador authored "The Gold Thieves" and "Memoirs of a Courtesan," the book cover pictured above, among dozens of other books and plays.)

Georges Bizet thought that El Arreglito was just an old folk melody, and ripe for the borrowing. At the last minute he found out that it actually was a published song, and then in the vocal score for his opera "Carmen," he gave credit to Sebastien Yradier. You may have heard Yradier's beautiful song "Paloma" another Habanera (often done as a Tango). Yradier learned these forms on a trip to Cuba in 1861. So in this cross-cultural song: "Carmen's Habanera," Bizet was imagining a Spanish melody of a Spanish composer who was imagining Havana, Cuba, in the Caribbean, in the New World! Continuing the cultural research, Cuban music is both African and Spanish! The moral to this story is: Keep it alive, write it down. Pass it along, and you may be able to get the credit for it!

Create a Time Capsule for the Future

Music allows you to capture a feeling, document a time and place, paint a picture - sometimes better than the visual arts. Music is a language that sometimes says things that words simply can't communicate. Make your experience eternal by writing it down. Let us continue to thank those that have upheld traditions, carried on culture, language, forms and feelings that would have otherwise been neglected, and sometimes even sadly lost forever.

Be the proud upholder of traditions by writing down your wonderful songs, feelings, dances, wisdom, words and sounds. In addition, exploring the depths of emotions shared in music helps us understand our own feelings more.

Affirmatinas – Positive Message Music

Music is often employed to help remember things. It is said that Hawaiian chants will recall 20 generations of names. The song we sing to learn the A-B-C's helps remember the alphabet. It is the same song that we call Twinkle Twinkle Little Star, and early in this book we help you make your own positive affirmation song out of it.

In our section on clave patterns we show you a positive message song phrase: **"Peace, ease and clarity – for me!"** This is a powerful positive message.

Bossanova Etude No. 1 (Lost In Love)

Teo Vincent IV
(c) 2011

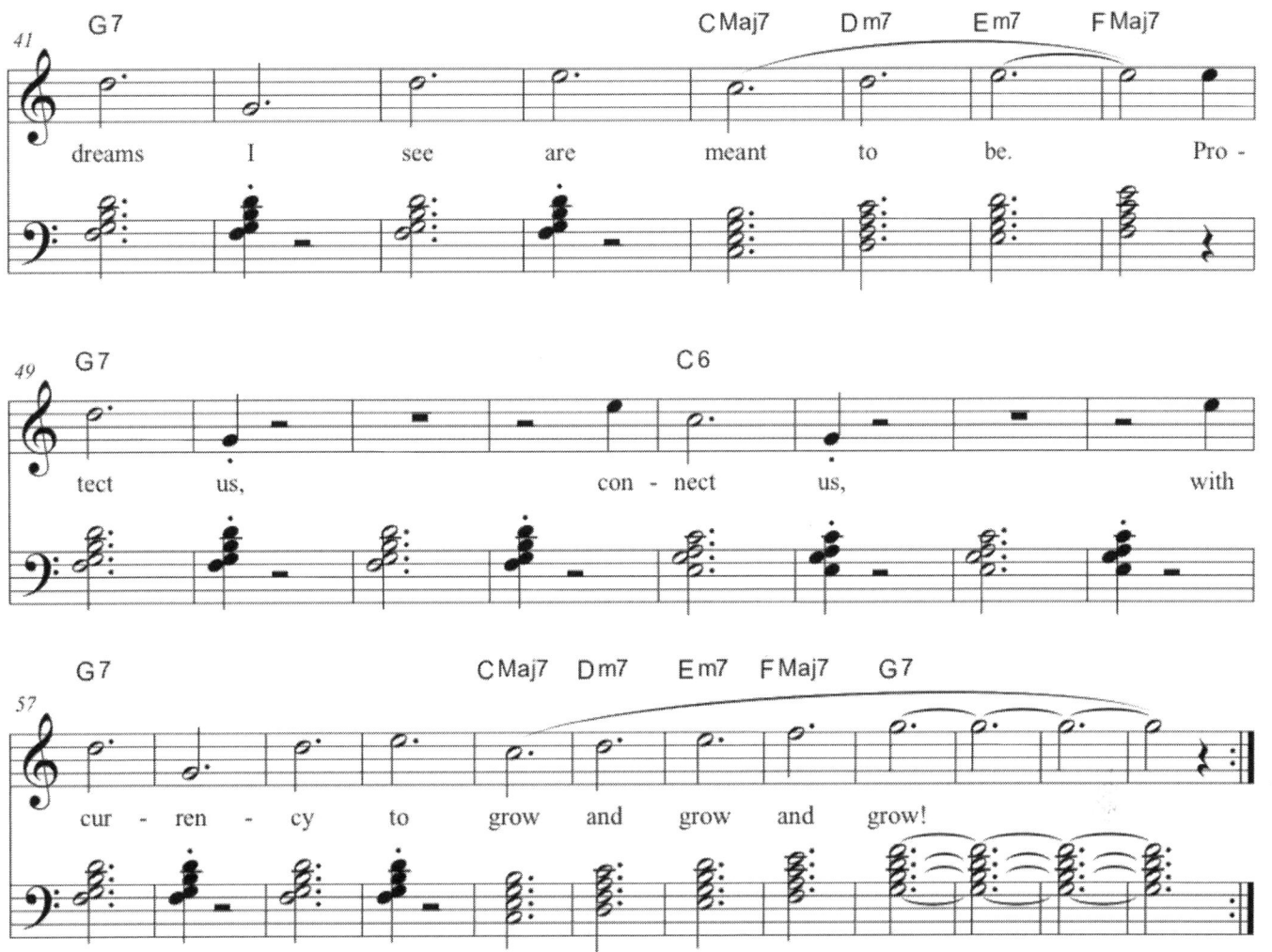

Lyrics of "Pati, to Patience" and "Silent Tears"

Pati (to patience)

All things change, nothing stays the same, you can only be, your highest aspirations. Every-thing changes, no-thing stays the same, (but) I'll always be, me. Bridge: Time - is like a knife, it cuts - things in and out of your life. If you, can learn to ride, time's ebb and tide, you will be free.

Silent Tears

I used to feel, oh so bad, I used to worry about all the people who feel sad. I used to be... so concerned with everything. Then one day it struck me, positivity is the way. I found a lot of people don't know that, and it just became my own way. So I paint a nice big smile on my face, and live the knowledge that I can live in Grace. Live in Grace. I like to go, into my own inner space, deep in my soul. I like to go into my special sacred space, where I have control. I like to go, deep inside where my heart says so, where my feelings can flow, where my spirit likes to go, deep into my soul.

As we stated earlier: *"There are many feelings that can't be expressed in words but music is the perfect medium to get the listener involved."* Music can set a tone, give you strength to stay focused and overcome challenges, impart deepest feeling, inspire greatness and bring back the most beautiful of memories, all in a flash!

One of the best things about music, and all art, is it's ability to help: ***Art can transmute suffering.***

Positive Messages on Classical Derivatives

In the ancient days to memorize a speech, the Greeks would associate parts of the speech with items in their house. This way, to recite their speech they simply visualized walking through their own house, something they couldn't ever forget how to do.

A wonderful technique to 1) put melodies squarely in your memory and 2) attach the beauty of masterful composer's works to your ideas, is this: Creative libretto to classical songs.

Though we can rave about the virtues of doing this, we also have to cry loud and strongly to stay appropriate in changing classical songs! This is wonderfully creative to do, but can be very disrespectful if done wrong.

One could even say that the masters were all mixing music and making variations on each other's songs all the time. This is true to a great extent, but this all just proves the following more and more:

You need to know the rules very well to know how to break them. Otherwise you are just making a terrible mess.

Honor the great composer that went before you, one fine way is to call the derivative by the original name, or call it variations on a theme. There is one technique that will get you out of a big mess!

Creating medleys, making themes such as "beds" or "jingles" can be done right and really be wonderful! Be careful and I'm sure you will make the great composers smile and enjoy your renditions, not roll over!

As you know, we believe, as the title of Vincent's first book states, in: "Honoring Those That Went Before!"

HONORING THOSE THAT WENT BEFORE

CLASSICAL & WORLD MUSIC
PIANO SCORES

TEO VINCENT IV

I Manifest My Destiny

Chopin-Dyer-Vincent

Frédéric Chopin's Mazurka in C, Wayne Dyer's book Manifest Your Destiny, Teo Vincent's sense of humor.

ChopinMadeAWay

Chopin-Vincent

Let It Be's

Liszt-Vincent
2008 1128

Lyrics: Life can be, a won-drous thing to see if we just let it be.

Inspirations from The Masters

In keyboards there is a common way to say the keyboard that controls the others. It is called the "Master." In case you don't get where we are going with this, the other sound units that are controlled by it, yes, they are called "slaves." Mightn't it have been so much wiser to call them *Guru* and *followers* or *subordinates* or something else.

Some people raised in the United States in particular have a deep dislike of the words master and slave. On the other hand, when talking about a master craftsperson, a maestro, it is a completely different thing:

The Master has mastered their craft. If there is any slaving, it is the master's slaving away to be better and better. The sheer number of pages penned by hand by various composers is awesome! It is a refreshing idea that the word master that can have the connotation of being an inspiration; **a great role model!**

Master should be a word that makes one elated with the amazing ability that it describes. We should gladly follow masters, and our world is truly improved by the more masters that there are and the more that we follow genuine masters!

The experiences of the great composers teaches us so much, and their music speaks in ways that words simply can not. Let us be grandly inspired by those amazingly hard working masters of their arts.

Johann Sebastian (J.S.) Bach (1685-1750) from the long lineage of musical Bachs was not only a master composer but was more known in his day as an organist and he promoted a new tuning he called "wohltemperirt" that we call **well tempered** (which sounds like something we could use today in general as well). *Improving our tempers!* ☺

In some ways this tuning allowed people to play in any key. Before in "true tuning" instruments were only good for certain keys (like the Bb Trumpet or F French Horn).

Bach was quite the family man, truly *The Patriarch*. With 20 children he would have had to be most responsible, and working for the church, much of his genius was used in how to make the old chorales exciting and more interesting (for which some complained).

He was also a gatherer of the ancient forms and compiled many songs into Suites. English and French Suites brought beautiful folk forms into an elegant performance style for his patrons. In 1717 he was offered a position in Cöthen but the Duke of Weimar had Bach locked up for a month before was liberated and allowed to go work for the more open-minded Prince Leopold (see the 1995 video "Bach's Fight for Freedom.")

Georg Friedrich Händel (1685-1759), later George Frideric Handel, was another Master of the Baroque period. His father died in 1697 at the age of 74, leaving him as the "man of the household" when he was 12. Later Handel traveled widely, enjoyed great success in Italy, including visiting the Medicis. He was hired by German prince George Elector of Hanover (who became King George I of England) but stayed in Italy for 2 years before coming to Britain to his work!

The King and Handel were reconciled because he loved "Water Music" so much that he had it played 3 times!

Handel wrote the oratorio "Messiah" which benefited the Foundling Hospital in London. He eventually became a British citizen and was buried in Westminster Abbey. Though he and Bach never met, they both had studied Fugues and other music with the master of masters, Dieterich Buxtehude (1637-1707).

Each took the hand that they were dealt (whatever the life difficulties, opportunities and obligations), and created a positive, beneficial finale. This is one of the key ideas regarding taking inspiration from the masters.

The first harpsichord of Franz Joseph Haydn (1732-1809) was said to be "worm eaten," he had many odd jobs such as street serenader, and valet, but went on to become Father of the Symphony, Father of the String Quartet, not to mention being Beethoven's music teacher and Mozart's close friend.

Thanks to Nadezhda Filaretovna von Meck (1831-1894) for sponsoring both Pyotr Ilyich Tchaikovsky (1840-1893) and Claude-Achille Debussy (1862-1918). Just think how much beautiful music is because of Baroness von Meck!

Music is the Universal Language

The Universal Language of Music owes a debt of gratitude to its greatest writers. Ludwig van Beethoven (1770-1827) may have had more emotional experiences than we would ever wish for. The longing of Frédéric François Chopin (1810-1849) for his dear Poland was more than one could bear. He cried into his piano each night, and the tears become sparkles of brilliance, uplifting grace and transcendence.

Let your ears be your guides, your teachers, and even your refuge. Thank you so dearly, great masters, for sharing your notes, your emotings and emotions…

Use stories of the great composers (and performers) to learn how to be more successful as a composer (or performer) in this world, here and now. Follow the best examples of composer's achievements.

Franz Liszt (1811-1886) was very well connected. He used his influence and was a great benefactor to other composers such as Robert Alexander Schumann (1810-1856), Hector Berlioz, (1803-1869), Wilhelm Richard Wagner (1813-1883), Joseph-Maurice Ravel (1875-1937), Chopin, Debussy and others.

Liszt was known to not only teach many great musicians for free, but helped so many financially! He did benefits for a Beethoven statue, and he also transcribed Beethoven's 9 symphonies for piano. This was no easy task because there were none of the technologies we have available nowadays!

Chopin and Liszt dedicated many great songs and studies to each other. Liszt brought gypsy music to the classical stage, as well as many other forms, styles and genres he invented, pioneered and used his vision to share with us.

Brahms created many great orchestral versions of wonderful folk music. His Hungarian Dances are amazing! Many great composers took the time and effort to take folk musics, even gypsy musics and write them down – as difficult as that must have been, writing down the special techniques that ethnic and folk musicians have.

Beware some of the things that Schubert did that weren't good for his musical future. You could say he simply ran with the wrong crowd. Still, let us be inspired by the way he composed so much beautiful music even having come from abject poverty!

Not one of Schubert's symphonies was played in his lifetime, and they are some of the most well loved symphonies of all time. Thank you dearly Franz Schubert for sharing your beautiful music with us all!

Another amazing musician who came from poverty was Antonio Salieri (1750-1825).

The well-known movie Amadeus paints a wrong picture. It portrays Wolfgang Amadeus Mozart (1756-1791) as a brat and Salieri as his murderer. Both of those fictional depictions are the farthest you can get from the truth – and extremely insulting to two musical giants, geniuses who haven't been outdone on this planet ever since! Salieri taught Beethoven, Schubert and many others. Let us appreciate him.

Sure it is sad to know that Mozart in his 35 years could have done more if he had lived longer. But on the other hand look at this: All the symphonies, concertos, sonatas, operas, quartets, and many other forms that he produced, these were all in his own hand! Think how many pages every day he must have produced.

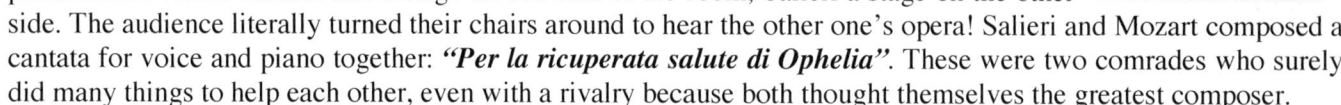

Mozart was so prolific and amazing that even in that short time he has produced so much music that in many ways he still has no equal or superior.

In reality Salieri and Mozart were brothers in the Masonic lodge. There was one performance where Mozart had a stage on one side of the room, Salieri a stage on the other side. The audience literally turned their chairs around to hear the other one's opera! Salieri and Mozart composed a cantata for voice and piano together: *"Per la ricuperata salute di Ophelia"*. These were two comrades who surely did many things to help each other, even with a rivalry because both thought themselves the greatest composer.

Joseph Boulogne (1733-1799) was the amazing African and French composer known as Chevalier de Saint-Georges, often called "The Black Mozart." Some say Mozart copied a musical line from him to use in a ballet, but in those days it was a great compliment, a respectful thing, to quote another great composer.

Just as Chopin built virtuoso piano compositions on Mozart's "Magic Flute" opera, and Liszt built heavily on other's great works, let us build from fantastic foundations to elevate them, and ourselves and all who hear it.

You need to know the rules very well to know how to break them; otherwise you are just making a terrible mess!

Honor the great composer that went before you. One fine way is to call your derivative by the original name, or call it variations on a theme. That is one technique that will get you out of a big mess.

Creating medleys, making themes such as "beds" (background music for talk over) or "jingles" can be done right and be wonderful. Be careful and surely you will make the great composers smile and enjoy your renditions of their works, not roll over!

May the great musical masters inspire the best in you!

Map your life out based on the successes and joys of your favorite composers and artists. Watching videos about great artists such as Beethoven, Chopin, Liszt, Mozart, Bach and so on, these will give you a keen insight into how to be successful in your own arts!

See how your hyper-creative and uniquely-innovative abilities can be used productively in the world, instead of making you feel left-out or different. Learn how incredibly gifted artists took full advantage of their gifts and have graciously produced them in ways so that we can fully enjoy them even hundreds of years later!

Lift yourself to the highest aspirations that you have. Live in the knowledge that raising yourself and being inspired by greatness may have solitary times, even lonely periods – especially such as endless practicing!

The rewards of pushing yourself to follow examples of highly productive artists are indescribable, and priceless.

Did you guess whose pictures these were?
You should know most of them! OK they were: Gershwin, Tchaikovsky, the Bach family, Handel, Haydn, Beethoven, Liszt, Chopin, Schubert, Mozart, Liszt, Verdi, Clara & Robert Schumann.

ARTTSI Institute's Charmony Lessons Design

Harmony is balance and appropriateness. When we are in harmony things go right and clear. If we start from a disharmonious situation, we may need special tricks to force ourselves into harmony. Extra pushes help us be in balance regardless of situation. Our world is more open to diverse attitudes and styles. To embrace them well we should know the artistic functions of musics very different from ours. Useful and effective integration we at Givnology call *Synthegration*, appropriately synthesizing new things from very diverse elements.

Our goal is to help: 1) All of the schools that can't afford full music rooms, expensive equipment; 2) The vast number of out-of-work professional musicians who would love to share their skills back; and 3) The would-be-music students who aren't getting the normal exposure to what making music really is, and this way counter the artless and heartless world. **With our books we help to solve all of these issues perfectly!**

Musically this system is to help people who focus on rhythmic centers, emotional and intellectual centers all perform in unison, being in balance in our uni-verse. This means more rhythmic awareness for some, more emotional awareness for some, and more harmonic awareness for others.

Compassionate artists give a helpful hand to others to see how enriching, motivating and positive art can be. Great artists share a timeless gift, their experience with art which lives much longer than we do, and is ever growing.

The incredible joy of knowing music, how it is made, how it is written, and how it is played, enriches our lives in priceless ways. How artists share their experiences with us, across time, languages and cultures, is no less than magic. Helping youth, or even young-at-heart people to experience the magic of music is a great ability to share.

This study system is designed to be useful many-fold: 1) As a reference of instrument ranges and transpositions it helps composing. 2) As a rhythmic percussion curriculum it allows everyone to improve timing, tempo, and the ability to play music together. 3) For fun and beautiful music lessons for yourself. **You (and your ears) are your best teacher!** Make your musical journey a fun exciting trip and you will have countless hours enjoying it.

Many years of experience in teaching, performing, writing and band-leading have been condensed into handy reference materials, and step-by-step lessons that can be easy to follow, improve music understanding and appreciation. In this book are germs, seeds that can be expanded into lessons in many directions.

We are upholding traditions, sacred artistic knowledge and cultures. Hopefully you will continue keeping the art and culture alive by enjoying being another vehicle for it. *May you enjoy carrying on the great traditions!*

Havah Nagilah in Modes:
(this way you can then play it in any key!)

{V V V V i i V-iv V} *fine*
{V V iv iv iv iv V-iv V}
i i i-iv6 i-iv6
{i-i7 VI-i} {iv6-V7 iv6}
Vø V7 i i D.C. al *fine*

Chamber Concerto in D major, RV 93 (2)

Che Farò Senza Euridice?

Christoph Willibald Gluck 1714-1787
Theme Reduction (c) 2014 Teo Vincent IV

World Music Compilation 82

L'Inverno (Winter) from Quattro Stagioni (The 4 Seasons)

Antonio Vivaldi 1678-1741
(c) 2015 Teo Vincent IV

World Music Compilation 83

Aria del Piacere, Il Trionfo del Tempo e del Disanganno
Pleasure's Aria, The Triumph of Truth and Time

George Frederic Handel
1685-1789 (c) 2011 Givnology

Lyrics:
Lascia la spina cogli la rosa tu vai cercando il tuo dolor, tu vai cercando, tu vai cercando il tuo dolor. Lascia la spina cogli la rosa tu vai cercando tuo dolor.

World Music Compilation 84

Aria del Piacere
Lascia la spina, cogli la rosa, tu vai cercando il tuo dolor. Canuta brina, per mano ascosa, guingera quando nol crede il cor.
Pleasure's Aria
Leave the thorn, pluck the rose, you are seeking your own sorrow. An unseen hand will bring you hoary old age ere your heart imagines.

Les Baricades Misterieuses

Gelido in Ogni Vena
from the opera Farnace

Antonio Vivaldi (1678-1741)
(c) 2011 Givnology

Farnace (play by Antonio Maria Lucchini), Music: Antonio Vivaldi 1678-1741

Gelido in ogni vena scorrer mi sento il sangue, l'ombra del figlio enangue m'ingombra di terror.

I feel my blood like ice coursing through every vein. The shade of my lifeless son afflicts me with terror.

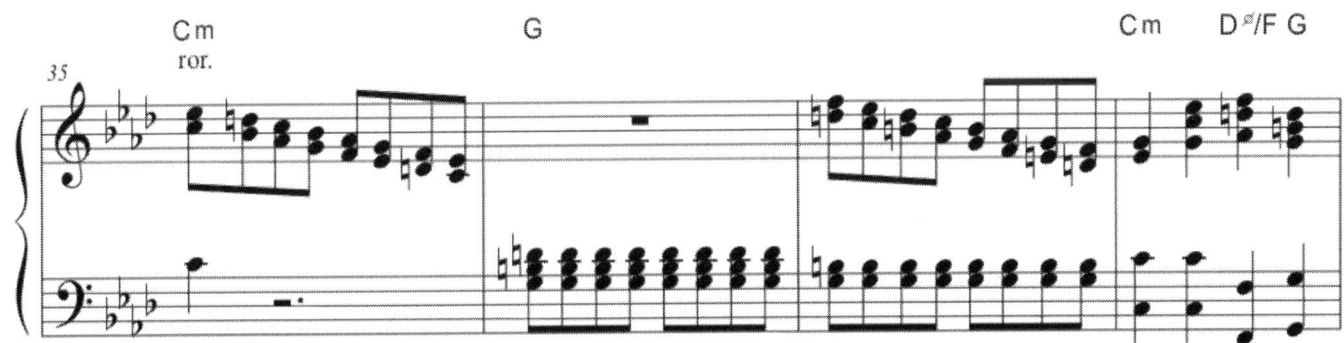

Gelido in Ogni Vena (3)

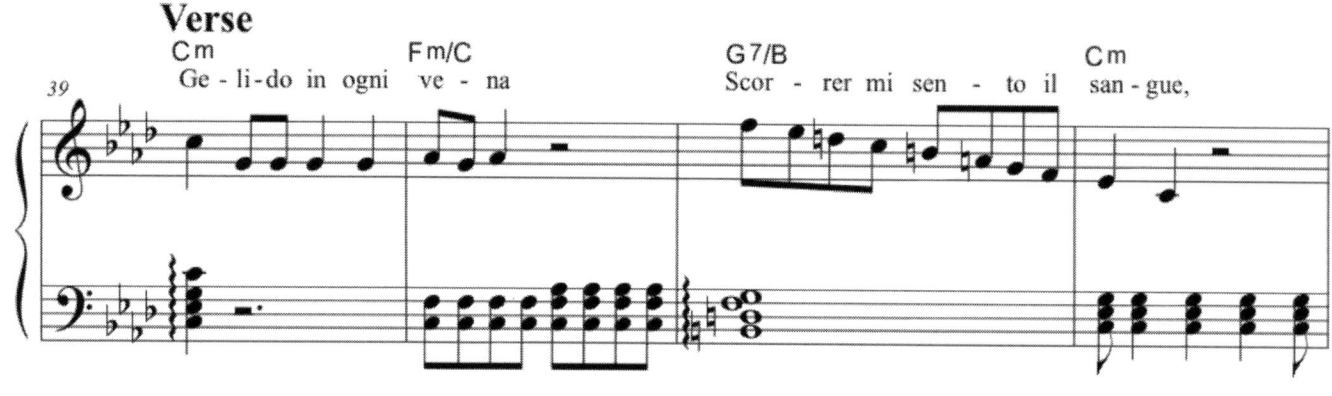

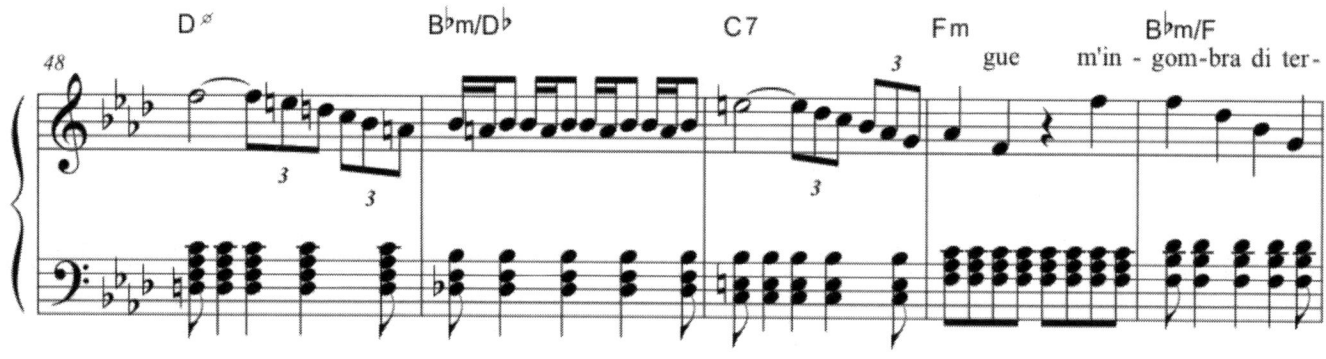

Song To The Moon
from the opera Rusalka

Antonin Leopold Dvorak
(1841-1904)

Bars 6 and 14 Cb/Ab can be thought of as Abm7

Clarinet Concerto in A Major

Wolfgang Amadeus Mozart (1756-1791)
Piano Reduction (c)2011 05 Teo Vincent IV

Adagio

Clarinet Concerto in A Major page 2

Ave Maria / Ellens Gesang
Opus 52 #6
Franz Schubert (1797-1828)
Layout (c) 2011Givnology

World Music Compilation 98

Casta Diva

from the opera **Norma**, Opus 61

Vincenzo Bellini (1801-1835)
(c) Givnology 2011

World Music Compilation 100

Casta Diva page 2

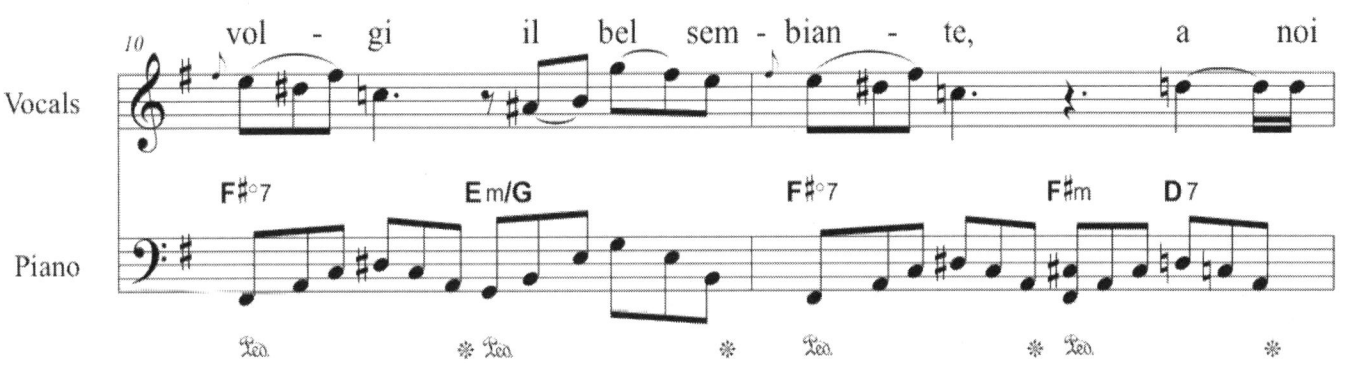

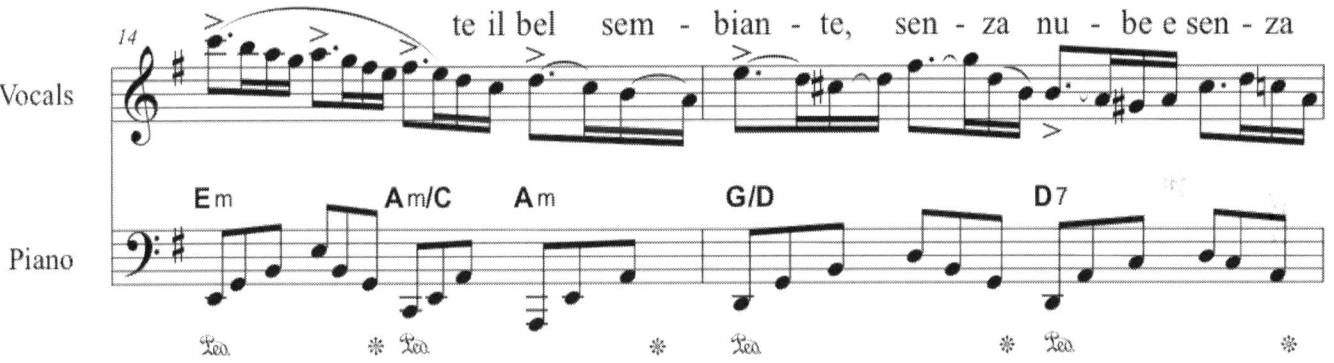

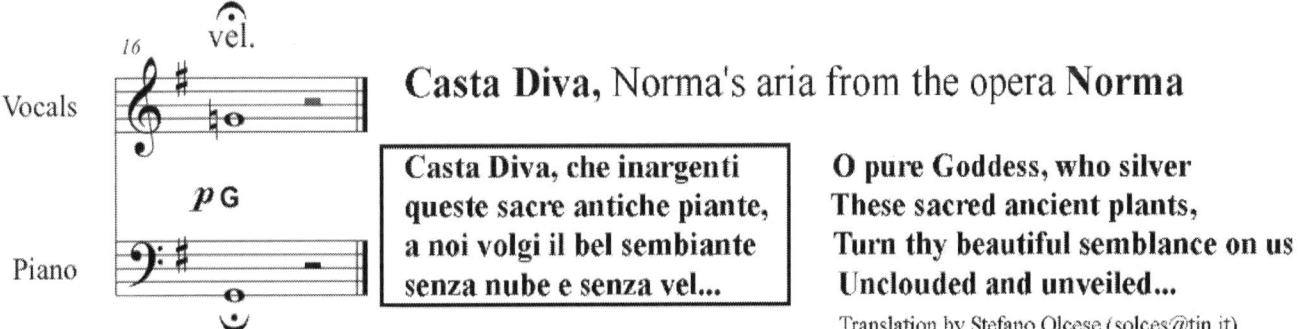

Casta Diva, Norma's aria from the opera **Norma**

Casta Diva, che inargenti
queste sacre antiche piante,
a noi volgi il bel sembiante
senza nube e senza vel...

O pure Goddess, who silver
These sacred ancient plants,
Turn thy beautiful semblance on us
Unclouded and unveiled...

Translation by Stefano Olcese (solces@tin.it)

Symphony #9 Andante moderato

Ludwig Van Beethoven
(c) 2013 Teo Vincent IV

World Music Compilation 102

Bizet Symphony #1 Adagio

Georges Bizet 1838-1975
(c) Teo Vincent IV 2013 0405

World Music Compilation 103

Romeo And Juliet Overture

Pyotr Ilytch Tchaikovsky (1840-1893)
© Teo Vincent IV 2011

World Music Compilation 104

Andalucia from Suite Española

Ernesto Lecuona 1895-1963
(c) 2011 Givnology

World Music Compilation 105

Glossary of Italian Musical Terms for Performance Instruction

a tempo: in time

Adagio brillante: Slowly with brilliance

Allegretto cantabile: cheerfully, in a singing style

Allegro capriccioso: lively & playful

Allegro con brio: with brilliance

Allegro con molto ritmico: with a lot of rhythm

Allegro giusto: steady timing

Allegro vivace: lively

Andante cantibile: in a singing style

Andante, tempo giusto: strict, exact time

Andantino placido: moderate & tranquil

brillante: with brilliance

con spirito: with spirit

delicato e amoroso: delicately & lovingly

dolce con espressivo: sweet & expressive

dolce con grazia: sweet & gracefully

dolcissimo: very sweet

Giocoso: playful

Grandioso e scherzando: grandly & playfully

legato, ma con brio: sustained, but with brilliance

Marcato e misterioso: emphasized & spooky

Moderato con affetto: affectionately

Moderato tranquillo

molto ritmico: with much rhythm

piu serioso: more serious

Presto giocoso: quick & playful

ritardando e ritardando: slower & slower

sempre mp: same volume

smorzando: softer and softer

tempo giusto: exact timing

tranquillo: peaceful

Vivace a capriccio: lively and funny

The Total Musical Piece

Having found the correct way to compliment the rhythmic phrases, and how to be in harmony with the chord structure, the musical pieces all fall together perfectly.

We not only have all sections rehearsed and ready to integrate together just right, or "synthegrate," but at the point where performance is coming up and all these loose ends are tightened up, one can think of the higher goals achieved by performing all together, as one.

The entire group, congealed to be one sound, one essence, is the greatest example of us all being one. At this point we have, pun intended, **musical peace**.

Memorable words have been put with the percussion to make the songs fun, positive, and easy to remember.

These are the final exams if this is a school music course, or fun performances that can include all people, all roles, *dancing and costumes too!*

> *It is truly great, when the individuals and individual sections have all practiced, and coming together can be a joy of finding ways to synchronize the steps, movements around the performing area, and even nuances such as winks and joyful gestures –*
>
> *this is where one is fully self-actualized and experiences being beyond their own body, and their own time and place – in the most beautiful sharing ways!*

This is the truest meaning of upholding traditions and keeping cultures alive. A great sense of belonging happens. We unite to truly become a larger one, much more than just the sum of the parts.

The Music Is Alive!

and

1!

The melody has been shifted 2 beats to help teach clave and palito (little sticks) patterns.
It is a good lesson to play "binary" back and forth between 1. Clave (& downbeat on Agogo) and 2. Palito with both hands. For the advanced: keep switching the hands of the patterns.
Any flat piece of wood makes a good wood block for practice, find a safe-to-hit piece of metal for an agogo/cowbell sound. Wood block is a common American instrument for clave type parts.

Yemaya is the Yoruba tribe from Nigeria's Ocean Goddess
A "Bembe" is a drumming, singing and dancing ritual
"Coro" means chorus in Spanish and Italian
These are "Layered Rhythms," (some parts may feel 3/4)
The form goes back and forth between these 2 percussion patterns: the top system of staves is an intro pattern, the second and third systems have the full bembe agogo pattern

World Music Compilation 112

World Music Compilation Table of Contents 2

The following 3 books are:

Vincent Trio Scores (2015), 16 Scores for a Bass-Piano-Violin Trio ISBN-13: 978-149610952   BISAC: Music / Songbooks

Carmen's Habanera from the opera Carmen, Opus 21 no. 2 by Georges Bizet (1838-1875) ------------ 114
Symphony Number 3 in F Major, Poco Allegretto, Opus 90 by Johannes Brahms (1833-1897) ------- 117
Komm Zigany from the operetta Countess Maritza, 1924 by Emmerich Kalman (1882-1953) --------- 122
Don Sanche's Aria from Don Sanche ou le Chateau d'Amour, Opus 1 by Franz Liszt (1811-1886) -- 129
Laudate Dominum, K339 by Wolfgang Amadeus Mozart (1856-1891) ----------------------------- 134
Piano Concerto No. 21, Andante, K467 by Wolfgang Amadeus Mozart -------------------------- 138
Piano Concerto No. 2, Adagio, Opus 18 by Serge Rachminoff (1873-1943) ----------------------- 147
Boléro from the ballet Fandango by Joseph-Maurice Ravel (1875-1937) ----------------------- -- 158
Bergamasca from Ancient Airs and Dances, Opus 40 by Ottorino Respighi (1879-1936) -------------- 163
Romanza Andaluza from Spanish Dances III, Opus 22 by Pablo de Sarasate (1844-1908) ------------- 170
Ave Maria / Ellens Gesang, Opus 52 no. 6 by Franz Schubert (1797-1828) and Franz Liszt ----------- 180
Serenade / Standchen (Schwanengesang D957 no. 4), Opus 134 / 90 no. 11 by Franz Schubert ------- 187
Piano Trio, Andante, Opus 17 by Clara Schumann (1819-1896) ------------------------------------- 191
Traumerei (Dreaming), Opus 15 no. 7 by Robert Schumann (1810-1856) --------------------------- 198
Fruhlingsstimmen (Voices of Spring) Opus 410 by Johann Strauss, Jr. (1825-1899) -------------------- 200
Ball, Opus 38 no. 3 by Pyotr Ilyitch Tchaikovsky (1840-1893) ------------------------------------- 204

Soul + Salsa = Soulsa Soft Latin Jazz Soul ISBN-13: 978-1496115171 BISAC: Music / Genres & Styles / Latin

Culture Crossing ------------------------------------- 209
Lost In Love --- 68
Montuno Etude No. 1 ------------------------------- 55
My Fantasy -- 214
Release To The Flow ------------------------------ 227
Swing Montuno ------------------------------------- 56
Take Me Home -------------------------------------- 228
That Makes This Heaven -------------------------- 239
Universe Of Love ----------------------------------- 242
Yoruba Diasporas ----------------------------------- 40

Barry's Songs I Soul Brother & Love Child of the 1960s ISBN-13: 978-1496112989 BISAC: Music / Genres & Styles / Soul & R'n B

My Lost Sweetheart (1983) ------------------------- 248
Our Ecstasy (1981) ---------------------------------- 250
Guitar Jam (1901) ----------------------------------- 256
Love You Forever (1979) -------------------------- 258
Lilly (1976) -- 259
Don't Be Deceived (1976) ------------------------- 260
Bionic Boogie (1975) ------------------------------- 266
Venice Caprice No. 4 (1975) ----------------------- 268
Venice Caprice No. 3 "Pterodactyl" (1975) ------ 270
Venice Caprice No. 2 (1975) ----------------------- 275
Venice Caprice No. 1 (1974) ----------------------- 277
Medimate (1974) ------------------------------------ 280
Barry's First (1968) --------------------------------- 281

Birdclipart.com

Symphony No. 3 Poco Allegretto

Poco Allegro e espress.

Johannes Brahms (1833-1897)
(C) 2012 Teo Vincent IV

Symphony No. 3 Poco Allegretto page 2

Symphony No. 3 Poco Allegretto page 3

Symphony No. 3 Poco Allegretto page 5

World Music Compilation 121

Komm Zigany (Come Play, Gypsy) 1924

Emmerich Kalman (1882-1953)
Trio Score (c) 2013 Teo Vincent IV

Komm Zigany (Come Play, Gypsy) 2

Komm Zigany (Come Play, Gypsy) 3

Komm Zigany (Come Play, Gypsy) 4

Komm Zigany (Come Play, Gypsy) 5

Komm Zigany (Come Play, Gypsy) 6

Komm Zigany (Come Play, Gypsy) 7

Furioso

Don Sanche's Aria

Opus 1

Franz Liszt (1811-1886)
(c) 2011 Teo Vincent IV

Don Sanche's Aria 2

World Music Compilation 130

Don Sanche's Aria 3

Don Sanche's Aria 4

Laudate Dominum 2

World Music Compilation

Laudate Dominum 3

Laudate Dominum 4

Mozart's 21st Piano Concerto

Andante

Wolfgang Amadeus Mozart 1756-1791
(c) 2012 Teo Vincent IV

Mozart's 21st Piano Concerto (p2)

Mozart's 21st Piano Concerto (p3)

Mozart's 21st Piano Concerto (p4)

Mozart's 21st Piano Concerto (p5)

Mozart's 21st Piano Concerto (p7)

Mozart's 21st Piano Concerto (p8)

Mozart's 21st Piano Concerto (p9)

Sergei Rachmaninoff PC2 Adagio Opus 18

Sergei Rachmaninoff
Trio Score @ Teo Vincent IV 2013

Sergei Rachmaninoff PC2 Adagio page 3

Sergei Rachmaninoff PC2 Adagio page 4

Sergei Rachmaninoff PC2 Adagio page 9

Sergei Rachmaninoff PC2 Adagio page 11

Bolero, from the ballet Fandango 2

World Music Compilation 159

Bolero, from the ballet Fandango 3

Bolero, from the ballet Fandango 4

World Music Compilation 161

Bolero, from the ballet Fandango 5

Bergamasca
from Ancient Airs & Dances Op. 40

Ottorino Respighi (1879-1936)
(c) 2001 Teo Vincent IV

Bergamasca 2

Bergamasca 3

Bergamasca 4

Bergamasca 5

World Music Compilation

Bergamasca 6

Bergamasca 7

World Music Compilation 169

Romanza Andaluza Op. 22
from Spanish Dances III

Andantino

Pablo de Sarasate 1844-1908
(2012) Teo Vincent IV

World Music Compilation 170

Romanza Andaluza

Romanza Andaluza (p4)

Romanza Andaluza (p6)

Romanza Andaluza (p7)

Romanza Andaluza (p8)

Romanza Andaluza (p9)

Romanza Andaluza (p10)

Ave Maria (Ellens Gesang) for Trio

Franz Schubert & Franz Liszt
Trio arrangement (c) 2011 Teo Vincent IV

Ave Maria (Ellens Gesang) for Trio 2

World Music Compilation 181

Ave Maria (Ellens Gesang) for Trio

Ave Maria (Ellens Gesang) for Trio 4

Ave Maria (Ellens Gesang) for Trio 5

Ave Maria (Ellens Gesang) for Trio 6

World Music Compilation 185

Ave Maria (Ellens Gesang) for Trio

Serenade 2

World Music Compilation 188

Serenade 3

Serenade 4

Piano Trio in G Minor Opus 17, Andante

Clara Schumann (1819-1896)
Trio Score (c) 2014 Teo Vincent IV

Note: with so many accidentals, including every single courtesy accidental would be cumbersome and confusing.

Clara Schumann Piano Trio in G Minor, Andante (2)

Clara Schumann Piano Trio in G Minor, Andante (3)

Clara Schumann Piano Trio in G Minor, Andante (4)

Clara Schumann Piano Trio in G Minor, Andante (5)

Clara Schumann Piano Trio in G Minor, Andante (6)

Clara Schumann Piano Trio in G Minor, Andante (7)

Traumerei

(Dreaming) Op15, No. 7

Robert Schumann (1810-1856)
(c) 2011 Teo Vincent IV

Traumerei 2

Fruhlingsstimmen
(Voices of Spring) Op. 410

Johann Strauss, Jr. (1825-1899)

(c) 2011 Teo Vincent IV

World Music Compilation 200

Fruhlingsstimmen 2

Fruhlingsstimmen 3

Fruhlingsstimmen 4

Ball

Moderato

Pyotr Ilyitch Tchaikovsky (1840-1893)
(c) 2012 Teo Vincent IV

World Music Compilation 204

Culture Crossing

Medium Salsa Groove

Teo Vincent IV
(c) 2011

World Music Compilation 209

My Fantasy

Teo Barry Vincent
(c) 2011

Slow Salsa Groove

World Music Compilation 214

My Fantasy 2

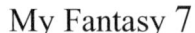

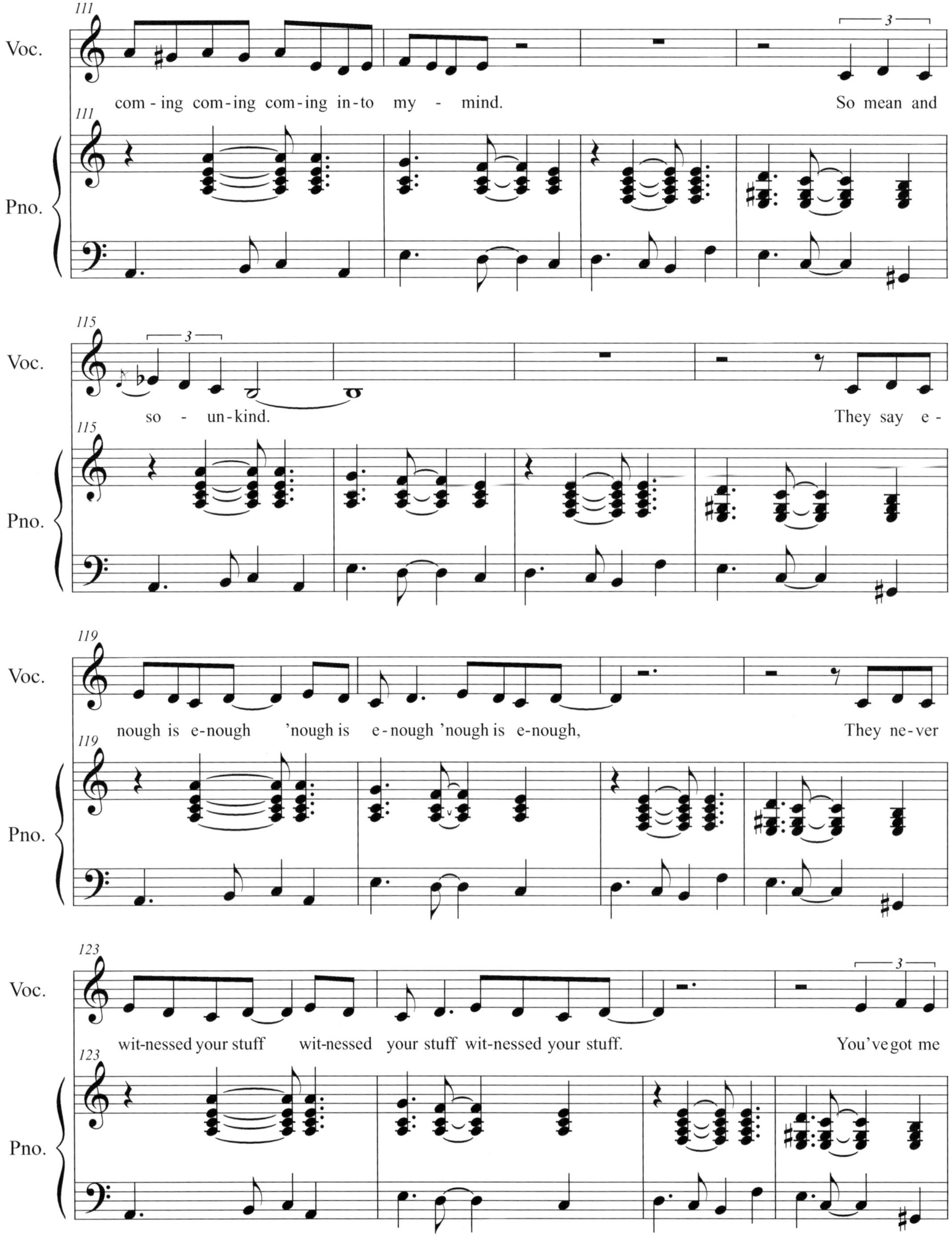
111
Voc.
com - ing com - ing com - ing in - to my - mind.
So mean and
Pno.
115
so - un - kind.
They say e -
119
nough is e - nough 'nough is e - nough 'nough is e - nough,
They ne - ver
123
wit - nessed your stuff wit - nessed your stuff wit - nessed your stuff.
You've got me

My Fantasy 10

My Fantasy 13

Release To The Flow

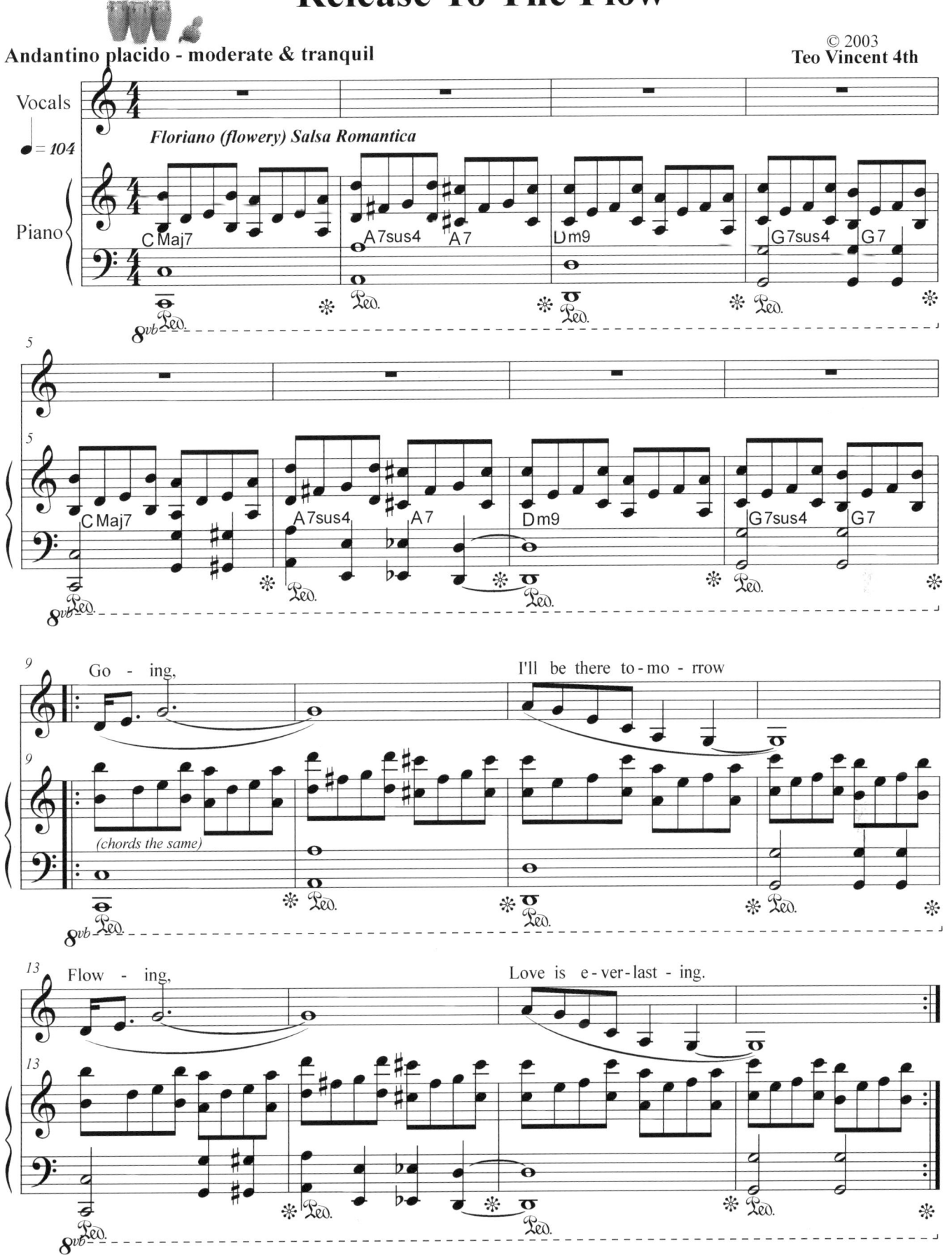

Release To The Flow (2)

Take Me Home

Take Me Home 2

World Music Compilation 232

81
Voc.
ne - ver for - get you, I'll ne - e - ver for - ge - - t yo - u,
Vln.
Keys
Bass
85
Fine
be - cause you ta - ke me home. I'll

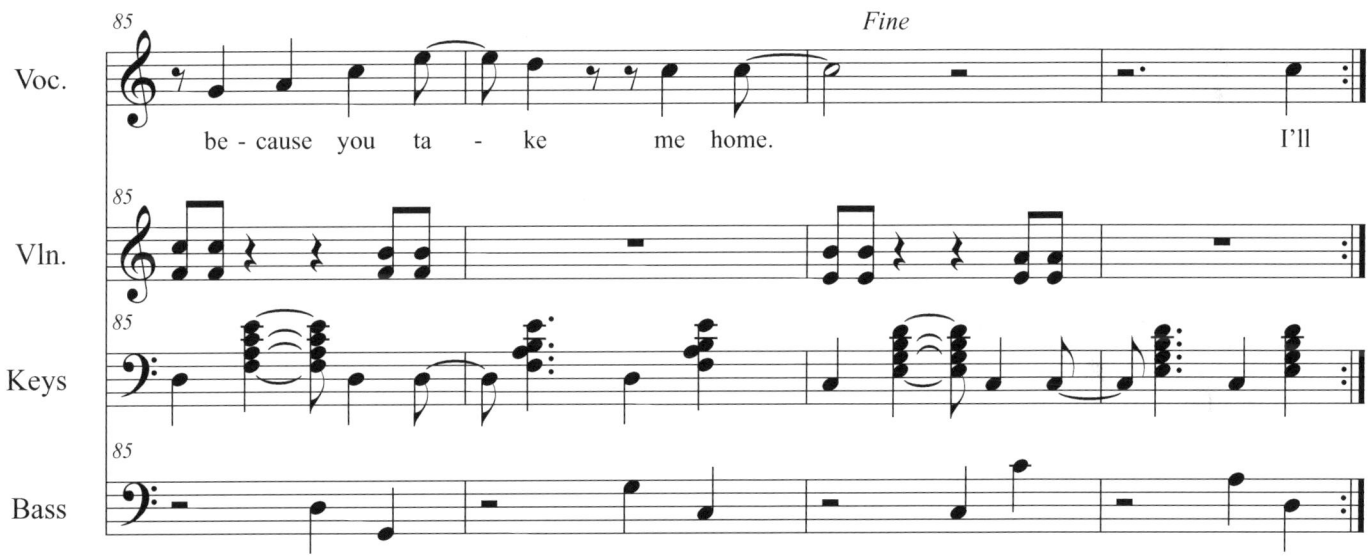

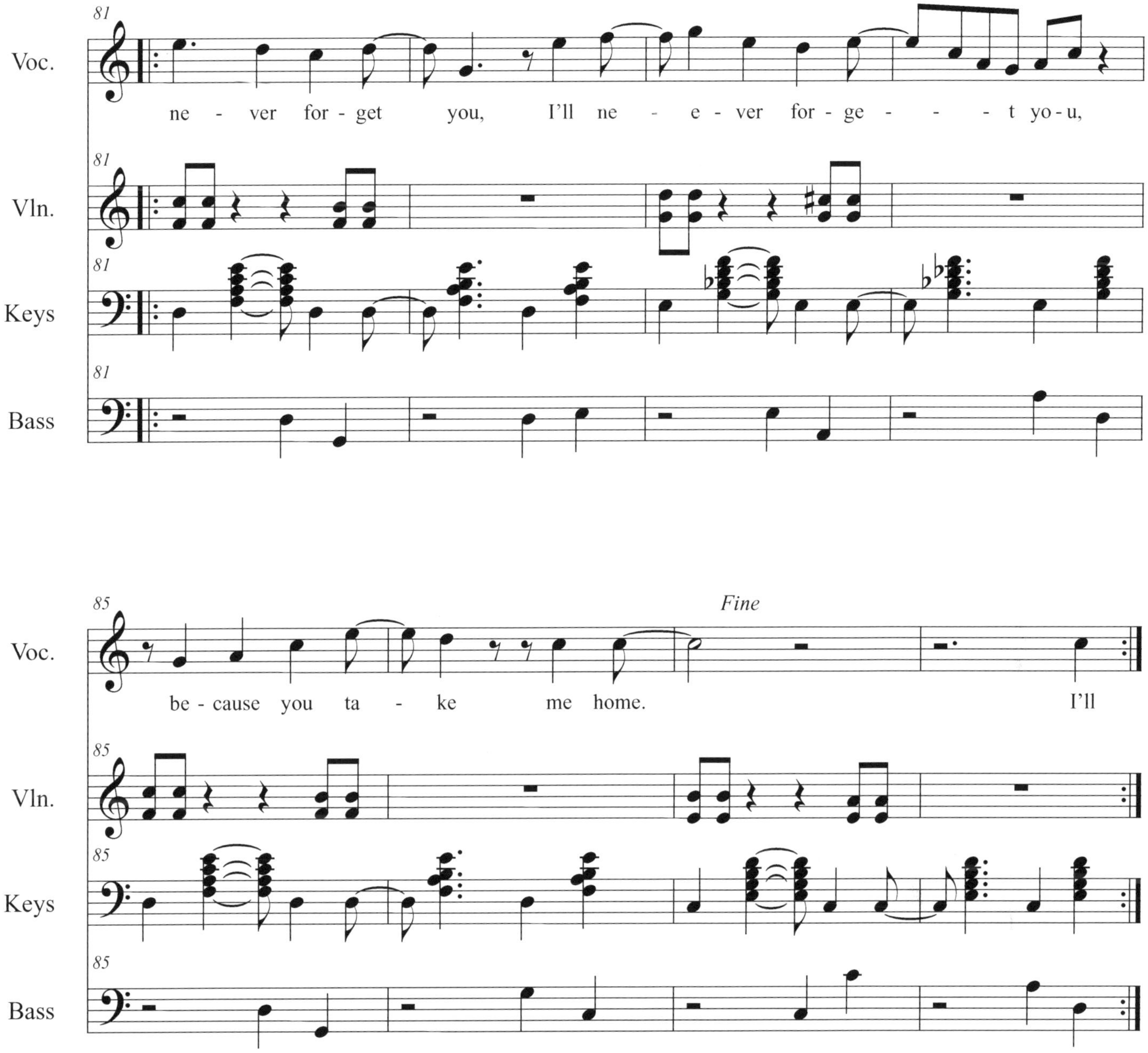

That Makes This Heaven page 4

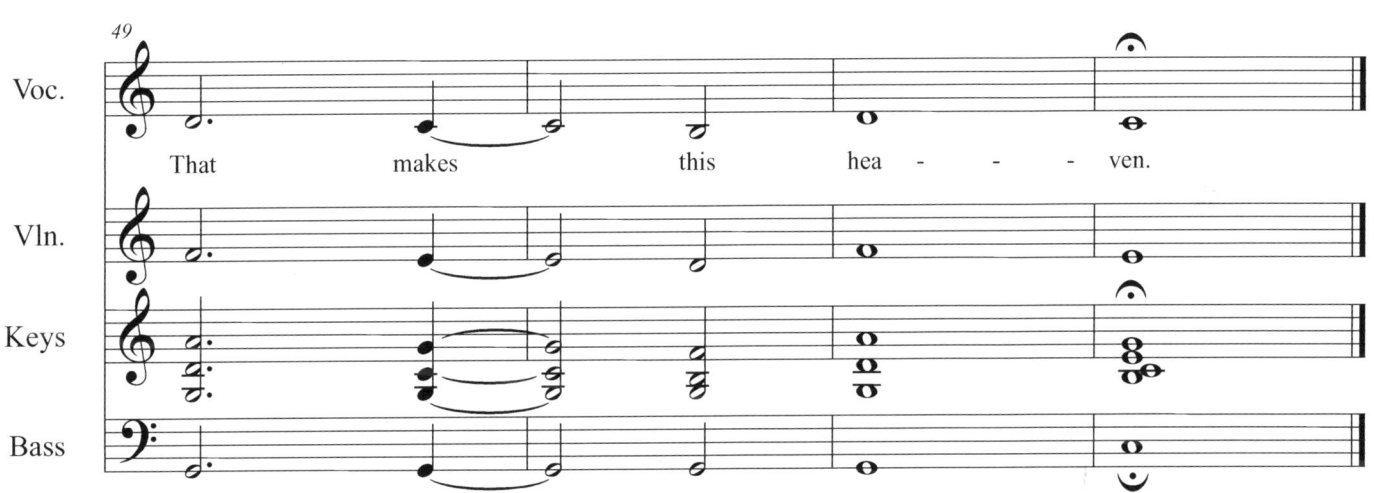

Cha Cha / Salsa Romantica

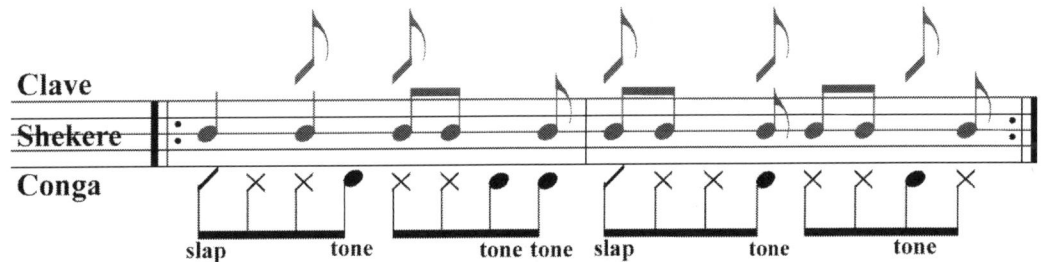

Universe of Love (2)

Our Ecstasy

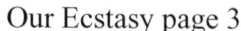

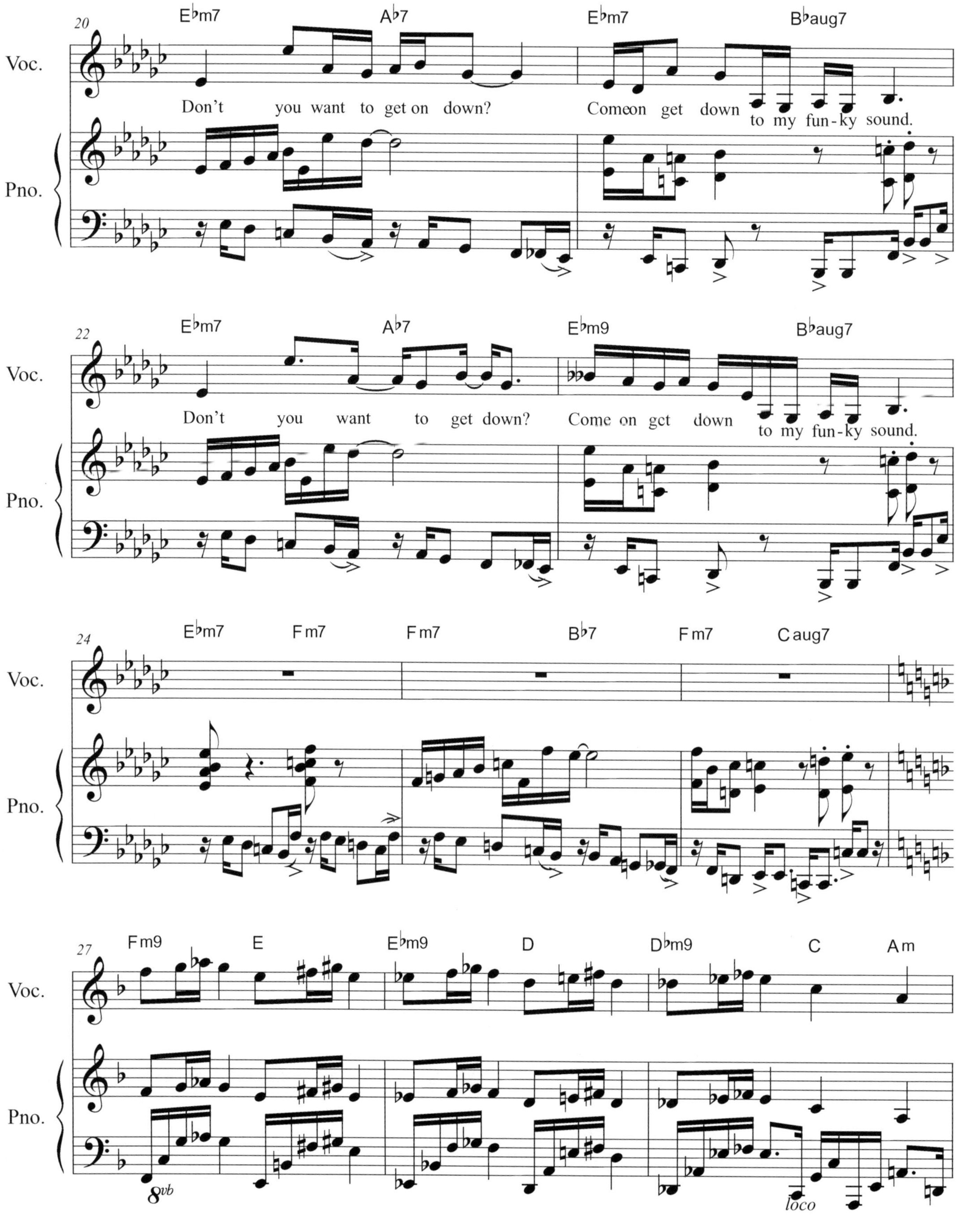
20
E♭m7 A♭7 E♭m7 B♭aug7
Voc.
Don't you want to get on down? Comeon get down to my fun-ky sound.
Pno.
22
E♭m7 A♭7 E♭m9 B♭aug7
Voc.
Don't you want to get down? Come on get down to my fun-ky sound.
Pno.
24
E♭m7 Fm7 Fm7 B♭7 Fm7 Caug7
Voc.
Pno.
27
Fm9 E E♭m9 D D♭m9 C Am
Voc.
Pno.
8vb
loco

Guitar Jam in Mi Dominant (E7)

T Barry Vincent
(c) Teo Vincent IV 2013

World Music Compilation 256

Guitar Jam in Mi Dominant (E7) page 2

Lilly's Song

Theodore Barry Vincent
(2012) Teo Vincent IV

Don't Be Deceived

Teo Barry Vincent
(c) 2011

Don't Be Deceived 5

Don't Be Deceived 6

Bionic Boogie

Teo Barry Vincent
(c) 2011

Head-throbbing beat

Bionic Boogie 2

*Loud and strong

* pinky plays f f# and G

Venice Caprice No. 4

Teo Barry Vincent
(c) 2011

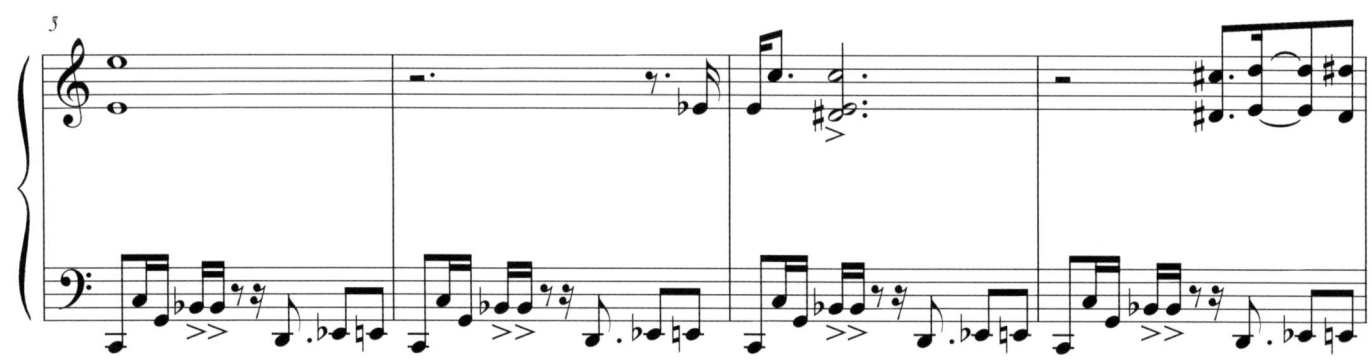

Venice Caprice No. 4 (2)

Venice Caprice No. 3
"Pterodactyl"

Teo Barry Vincent
(c) 2011

World Music Compilation 270

Venice Caprice No. 3 (2)

Venice Caprice No. 3 (4)

Venice Caprice No. 3 (5)

Venice Caprice No. 2

Teo Barry Vincent
(c) 2011

World Music Compilation 275

Venice Caprice No. 2 (2)

Venice Caprice No. 1

Teo Barry Vincent
(c) 2011

World Music Compilation 277

Venice Caprice No. 1 (2)

Venice Caprice No. 1 (3)

Opus 1

© 1968
Teo Vincent 4th

- Though written 3/4 it is played with a 6/8 compound time feel; the quarter note beat is constant.
- All chord's Bb's have a "courtesy accidental" to make it easier because it changes so frequently.
- Inspired by music of the whole world, my first song demonstrates both African Dance & Soul Music.

Manufactured by Amazon.ca
Bolton, ON